8/11

The publisher gratefully acknowledges the generous support of the Simpson Humanities Endowment Fund of the University of California Press Foundation.

SIMPSON

IMPRINT IN HUMANITIES

The humanities endowment
by Sharon Hanley Simpson and
Barclay Simpson honors
MURIEL CARTER HANLEY
whose intellect and sensitivity
have enriched the many lives
that she has touched.

Also by Michael McClure

ESSAYS, INTERVIEWS, BIOGRAPHY

Meat Science Essays
Wolf Net
Freewheelin Frank: Secretary of the Angels, as Told to Michael McClure
Scratching the Beat Surface: Essays on New Vision from Blake to Kerouac
Specks
Francesco Clemente: Testa Coda
Lighting the Corners: On Art, Nature, and the Visionary, Essays and Interviews

FICTION

The Mad Cub
The Adept

COLLABORATIONS

"Mercedes Benz," with Janis Joplin
Mandala Book, with Bruce Conner
The Adventures of a Novel, with Bruce Conner
Lie, Stand, Sit, Be Still, with Robert Graham
The Boobus and the Bunnyduck, with Jess
Deer Boy, with Hung Liu

FILMS, CDS, AND DVDS

Love Lion, with Ray Manzarek
The Third Mind, with Ray Manzarek
There's a Word, with Ray Manzarek
I Like Your Eyes Liberty, with Terry Riley
Rock Drill
Abstract Alchemist
Rebel Roar
Touching the Edge

DOCUMENTARIES

The Maze
September Blackberries

Of Indigo and Saffron

MICHAEL McCLURE

Of Indigo and Saffron

New and Selected Poems

EDITED AND WITH AN INTRODUCTION BY
Leslie Scalapino

 University of California Press   Berkeley Los Angeles London

University of California Press, one of the most distinguished univer-
sity presses in the United States, enriches lives around the world by
advancing scholarship in the humanities, social sciences, and natural
sciences. Its activities are supported by the UC Press Foundation
and by philanthropic contributions from individuals and institu-
tions. For more information, visit www.ucpress.edu.

University of California Press
Berkeley and Los Angeles, California

University of California Press, Ltd.
London, England

Library of Congress Cataloging-in-Publication Data

For acknowledgment of previous publication, please see credits,
page 311.

McClure, Michael.
    Of indigo and saffron : new and selected poems / Michael
McClure ; edited and with an introduction by Leslie Scalapino.
        p.   cm.
    Includes index.
    ISBN 978-0-520-26287-4 (cloth : alk. paper)
    I. Scalapino, Leslie. II. Title.
    PS3563.A262O38   2011
    811'.54—dc22   2010032585

Manufactured in the United States of America

20   19   18   17   16   15   14   13   12   11
10   9   8   7   6   5   4   3   2   1

This book is printed on Natures Book, which contains 50% post-
consumer waste and meets the minimum requirements of ANSI/
NISO Z39.48-1992 (R 1997) (*Permanence of Paper*).

For the protection of all beings

Contents

Preface

I want these poems to be soft and vigorous as the breath of a sparrow on the redwood deck rail and as tumultuous as a lion purring in the rain by the roadside in Kenya. These are poems from what love I have invented, what soul I have made, and the anger that has grown inside me at the biocidal war.

I have breathed the inspiration of countless many.

Introduction

The instant is the giant lamp we throw / our shadows by

LESLIE SCALAPINO

Michael McClure, renowned as a poet and playwright, and associated with the Beat Movement and San Francisco Renaissance, participated in the famous 1955 Six Gallery reading that inaugurated the Beat Movement. While noting the streamlining effect that eliminates difference by categorizing as movements individuals who are originating new gestures, McClure was living and writing alongside poets, artists, composers—dear friends—including (listing just a few): Philip Whalen, Gary Snyder, Allen Ginsberg, Robert Duncan, Bruce Conner, Robert Creeley, Amiri Baraka, Terry Riley, Francesco Clemente, Joan Brown, Wallace Berman, Jack Kerouac, Stan Brakhage, Jay Defeo, Joanne Kyger, and Jim Morrison.

McClure's *Josephine: The Mouse Singer* won an Obie for Best Play. *The Beard* and other plays, still performed, are regarded as seminal works of American theater. McClure is also an essayist, environmentalist, and lyricist (he wrote the lyrics, with Janis Joplin, for "Mercedes Benz"). He collaborates in performance of music and poetry with Ray Manzarek of The Doors. As collaborative dictation in conversation with Hells Angel Frank Reynolds, McClure transcribed Reynolds's autobiography, *Freewheelin Frank: Secretary of the Angels, as told to Michael McClure.*

Of Indigo and Saffron is a selection of McClure's poems, the earliest of which were published in 1956; the most recent, a new sequential poem, *Swirls in Asphalt*, was completed in 2008. This is not a traditional selected poems. It does not seek to represent the body of work of a poet by encapsulating the books in excerpts. Rather, my choice of poems was based on tracing certain gestures as related to vital elements in Michael McClure's poetry: particularly, a struggle evident in his work for apprehension of 'being' as that is (and is in relation to) language of poetry—as that language is *enactment of* 'being.'

Theater for Michael McClure is a seminal route of enactment (of live exchange); the gesture of his poetry is similar, a form of being in the instant. The line in a poem is trace of 'being' as speaking voice and as sense of sensation (what McClure called "writing the body"). This 'tracing' (as if reading body as mind/shape), sometimes tracing even the separation from oneself and from the instant, is akin to and uses as source Robert Creeley's poetry starting with *Le Fou*. McClure particularly loved *Pieces*. His recurrent gesture, which I would describe as 'split from one's own being, striving to be in it,' is comparable to Creeley's conflict, McClure's writing being simultaneous in time with Creeley rather than derived. McClure's early works track, and thus produce, a conflict as the means of *its* articulation, the sense of one being divided by language itself. His poems are sometimes an interior sense of division, conflict *equated* with its opposite (division is as if the same as—is in the same space as its opposite), conflict itself being simultaneity of being and time. McClure's sense of simultaneity is both union with the language and union with another person, the lover. The gesture of McClure's early poetry (such as *Hymns to St. Geryon* and *Dark Brown*) is the struggle to be actually *in* the time that one is *in:* at once present with oneself and with those who are loved.

> This is a war. The instant's
> history.
> (In the night I awoke and remembered you and you were gone
> though you lay by my side.
>
> "Yes Table"

In McClure's play *The Beard*, first performed in 1965–66 in San Francisco and Berkeley, the actor and actress, as the illusions/cultural icons of Billy the Kid and Jean Harlow in a field of "blue velvet eternity," as if exchange of words-insults that are also the actions between them, repeat these until in hypnotic trance the Kid goes down on Harlow (both clothed) in simulation of oral sex. The play had to be moved from the Fillmore Auditorium to a second venue in San Francisco, where the actors were arrested; the play then moved to Berkeley whose chief of police personally attempted to halt its performance. The actors were arrested the next day (the police thus avoided provoking the audience at the time of the performance). In 1968, during its run in L.A., the actors were arrested fourteen times. Subject of an obscenity trial challenging censorship laws, *The Beard* was charged with having "damaged society by inserting unlawful thoughts into the imaginations of others."[1]

Michael McClure creates a relation of his language to social one-dimensionality, which he defined as: "the individual in contemporary society has so little interior, individuated self remaining that the introjection of the values of society hardly fazes his consciousness. They *are* his consciousness. There is only one dimension."[2] In the one-dimensionality of such public officials as those who had halted the performances (mirrored in the one-dimensionality of Billy the Kid and Harlow as gargoyles, cartoon icons who are stars like light, physically beautiful Wrathful Deities), *The Beard* was interpreted as transgressing sexual taboos—in that, the play was not only suggesting a physical sexual act on stage, but also McClure's language makes a directly sexual subject be a sensory vehicle altering apprehension in the viewer (or reader). Rather than his language functioning to distance, which would be to regard reality as 'issues' or subjects exterior to the viewer/reader, sensation and at once *perceiving one's sensation* is recreated by the language (of *The Beard* and of his poems) so one is aware of oneself being action as phenomena. In *The Beard*, the senses are perceived *as* his language's hypnotic rhythm of repetition.

McClure's vehicle (especially in his early work) is blockage as *enactment* of our inherent contraries: Billy the Kid and Jean Harlow *are* violating social norms, for *both* are "Meat/Spirit" conjoining (only together they make a conversion) to *be* enactment, of love indistinguishable from one being a body. Robert Creeley commented on watching a rehearsal of *The Beard:* "Ask him how he *wrote* this extraordinary play—answer is he copied down words of the two people speaking in his head, conjoining to make poles positive. Wow."[3] McClure's language is a state or space in which conversion of destructive aspects of character can take place: *"Conversion will not come from denying inner impulses; only allowing them space to develop into their own negation will bring release from the pornographic loop."*[4] "Pornographic" (in reference to McClure's writing, which, obviously, can in no way be defined by that term) merely demonstrates the social barrier, the creating of duality.

In the poem "Rant Block," "Fakery of emotions.... Calling pure love lust to block myself" is McClure's use of barrier, inhibitions, the barrier stimulating its opposite, a flooding of one's awareness, same as the state of conversion in *The Beard* (that was to break the loop of pornography, as that is or may be one's own limitation of lust). Conversion is mysteriously a process as if *outside* him by only being produced in his language. His poem is a conversion in which its logic is only in the poem's sequence (its sequence is its shape—its shape is its sequence): its shape as language the illusion of mind-body split, by the sense of separation from oneself, figures a state of union also.

The readers of McClure's poems perceive as from their body outward— *to* the sense that body and mind (*there*, in reading the text) are the same. That is, the readers' seeing is to be *in* the instant of change as their sensation. One is also sometimes conscious, in reading, that one is in the poem as sensory experience, that of experiencing being *outside* of the phenomenal instant. That's what the CAPS are for. CAPS are one means of conveying consciousness of being inside and outside.

McClure's experience when he took peyote for the first time, the next day writing "Peyote Poem," of a lack of radiance that is phenomenal world as such, led him to the conception that warmth or love, in his particular sense of such, would need to be chosen or invented to be there (that is, radiance is a factor of the individual's choice):

> but accepting.
> The beautiful things are not of ourselves
>
> but I watch them. Among them.
>
> .   .   .   .
>
> in the bare room my stomach and I held together by dry
> warmth in space
> There is no reason for this! There is nothing but forms
> in emptiness — unugly
> and without beauty. It is that.
>
> I AM STANDING HERE MYSELF BY THE STOVE
> without reason or time.
>
> "Peyote Poem"

Language gesture as trace of sensory being in its relation to the instant, in McClure's poetry, is related to crisis: one is threatened with extinction as *seeing* in the one-dimensionality that's social seeing—and also as seeing (that was his peyote vision) as the coldness of phenomenal optical sight. To fall out of the instant (of event—of oneself, and of presence with those loved, the instant of being with others, at all) is not to be *in* oneself, as well as to be able to see others only as *they* are removed from the instant of *their* own being ("YOU ARE MY MEMORIES OF YOU") ("grafting nine"). Removed from one's instant, one would be only looking at reality from outside. Robert Creeley described McClure's artistic practice as "undistracted singularity."

This effort literally to *be*—and to observe the process of being—as possible only in the writing, is articulated in "Poem" from *Hymns to St. Geryon* (1959): "I wanted to turn to electricity—I needed/a catalyst to turn to pure fire." Later in "Crisis Blossom" (*Rain Mirror*, 1999): "'GIVE WAY OR BE SMITTEN INTO NOTHINGNESS/and everlasting night.' But I am here already./the tips of my fingers give off light." Later still, in *Plum Stones: Cartoons of No Heaven* (2002), McClure's tone is no less attentive but gentler: "WELCOME DEAR CHAOS" ("Plum Stone Fifteen").

Speaking-voice being itself phenomena: McClure noted that *Dark Brown* (1961), influenced by his plays, is as if the speaking voice creating the action that *is* event. The poem, *Dark Brown,* cites itself (text as) divided from action (an example of which is the poet's hand, in motion)—yet text is circular in its struggle (the text also being voice) to be an action: "*Say meat hand, the hand black/in the deed as the strain toward the act.*" In reading the text, it is as if a swatch of one's body were seen and experienced sensationally at once. Writing as speaking as being the act—in "Ode for Soft Voice," "we" are locked inside: "We move and never keep our forms but stare/at them address them as if they were there. This is my hand." The war that he delineates is the struggle (the reader's) to *be La Vita Nuova*—and to be *in* it (as in "The Chamber") by the force of being in its opposite: "*Vita Nuova*—No! The dead, dead, world." He's trying to activate time itself by being in it, the sense of this as if to counter his peyote experience of deadness. Deadness may be the consequence of societal, similar to phenomenal, coldness, as in "grafting twenty-seven": "*agathon kai kakon tauton,*' writes dark Herakleitos"—meaning "good and bad—the same."

Thus the present instant of/as reading, or exchange as speaking in the live moment of theater, is either struggle for—or acknowledged separation from—the instant, which is *Vita Nuova,* a form of *direct being* that as such would be also social reality. That is, *Vita Nuova,* to *be* (at all), has to, *now,* be our actual social reality.

Social one-dimensionality is substitution of given ways of thought in the place of the individuals' use of their faculty as their action of what McClure calls "intellectivity."[5] An example of defined knowing might be psychology, an intellectualized view accepted by the individual as if a given from the outside to describe their nature. He writes the origin of the split as counteraction to this social one-dimensionality: "The answer to joy is joy without feeling" ("Peyote Poem"). *Convention* of emotion is countermanded, emotion's negation *as* phenomenal coldness, in joy.

McClure first met Robert Duncan in 1954 by taking a class from him at

San Francisco State; the poems (which he'd written earlier and took to the class) were metrical, rhymed sonnets, sestinas, and villanelles. He remembers Duncan being somewhat alarmed by the fact of his apparently working in traditional forms. The mark of this formal interest is evident especially in McClure's early works such as *Dark Brown* and *Odes,* and is also evident in his countermanding given forms, as if in the same instant (of being form-ed) he's speaking to his own speaking: "There is no form but shape! no logic but sequence!/ . . . synaptic/stars/FORM IS AN EVASION!" ("Rant Block"). He writes awareness akin to Antonin Artaud (who was a source for McClure, as were Shelley, Blake, and Charles Olson) of being trapped inside a form (the human) that is both loose (transient) and rigorous in its relation to time: "This/is the war I battle in. This is the neverending instant./ . . . Never let them stand stemmed by form again" ("Rant Block"). The struggle also is an open innocence, as if formless, that is in *that* dual time: enacted (in the following) by his *seeing* the deer (dual, as necessitating being outside separated) at once with—at the same time as—he himself is afire, with/in human consciousness. Seeing, at all, is dual.

> Hey, deer, I'm on fire! You are more
> comfortable
> at some moments, because your spirit
> has fewer swirls and your conscious body
>
> lives deeper back in time.
>
> "To Glean the Livingness of Worlds"

Conception, formless, its language finding its own shape by the process of the language moving, related to text as the sense of body, sensational as that is *one's* mind also, is demonstrated by McClure's description of his first play, *The Blossom* (1960); the language of the play, as well as the spirit in which it was composed—of the text as whole-cloth from the imagination—is indicative of his work, akin I think to the poetics of "Rant Block" and to the poem sequence *Dark Brown:*

The play was written in a dream state. I went through a period of hypnotic suggestion, which I worked out with Sterling Bunnell. We had thought out a method which was a cross between hypnosis and auto-hypnosis, which he administered to me on some occasions previous to writing *The Blossom.* This was to plant the seed from which the play could grow—though I didn't write the play in a state of hypnosis. But it was while I was in a state that I saw the play being given birth to in my unconscious, where it formed as a stalactite—like a transparent stalactite of ice with the play inside it. And the stalactite fell onto a pink, moving floor and moved towards my consciousness! I wrote the play without changes—after sitting down to write a few days later.[6]

Performance of *The Blossom* was forbidden by the administration of the University of Wisconsin at Madison, which threatened to expel the student actors if the Drama Department went ahead with the staging of the play. A compromise was reached to allow one performance without announcement (so as not to reach an audience). The theater was packed. That McClure's writing shocked 'authorities' when it was first presented (in 1959, City Lights Books sold *Dark Brown* only under the counter to known customers), is interesting as our cultural history; most interesting is why that should be so. I think it is because McClure's writing is (still at present) startlingly the formless act of the reader/viewer's investigation of mind-shape: *visionary* is one's optical seeing and sensation. That is, it is '*real.*'

Ghost Tantras (1964), written in the period of McClure's experimentation with traditional forms, in playful spirit, is what McClure calls "beast language." Apparently without traditional forms (in the sense of not human language at all yet aping this), his text is part recognition, part imagined human words, to be not so much an *imitation* of beast language as melded with it, thus aware that *human* language is imitation. It suggests taking apart language at all (any), similar to such experiments and conceptions later in language poetry. In humor and speaking voice, human and beast sounds retain their identifying outlines as if they are in the 'middle' of each other, imagination and sounds 'figuring out' a new language partaking of both. Akin to this written gesture is a film for which McClure reads a poem six times, ending in word-roars, *grahhrs,* delivered in front of four lions in the lion house of the San Francisco Zoo. As he repeats *"grahhr,"* the lions ultimately are roused and begin roaring in reply.[7]

McClure described conceiving of reality in the Taoist sense, as an uncarved block, entities thus proportionless:

> What I'm speaking of is the Taoist notion that the universe that we perceive is an "uncarved block," that all time/space occurrences of the past, present, and future are one giant sculpture of which we're a part. It's not as if something is going to exist in the future or that something has happened in the past, but that it's all going on at once. And we're in it. If we're aware of that, there's a *proportionlessness* that is a liberating state or condition. If we understand that we're not of a particular "behemothness," then we sense that we're without time. When we have that experience, there's a peace and an understanding that can come over us. We can make better judgments and more positive actions.[8]

McClure's signature characteristic, of centering each line of a poem on the page without left or right border, is akin to, and elicits in reading, this sense of proportionlessness (of reality as uncarved block), in which conceptually (that is, at once sensationally) phenomena 'appear' (as in) to lose conventional fixed relation, either dimension or interaction.

This use of lines centered on the page, though seemingly the same form used in many of his poems, is a sensitive instrument making different inventions in different poems. The gesture of *Plum Stones: Cartoons of No Heaven* (2002) is mapping of momentary states as mind-shapes similar to states arising in one sitting meditation, as "uncarved block." A sense of the body's spine is as if in sensorial space as that is also page, centered lines of the poem: "STRAIGHT BACK/and/rising from pelvis/hands in a mudra./ Making a monkey" ("Plum Stone One"). "Monkey mind" is a Buddhist term for 'mind all over the place' playing tricks, rather than quiet-centered. "All is one carved into zero" ("Plum Stone One") is the state apprehended or imagined by the entire poem sequence as its *effect* (future), rather than reliance on that as the *subject* of the individual poems (of *Plum Stones*). The emptying out of mind-play to a state utterly open as such 'empty'/serene— is *first the poem,* rather than the poem *describing* a prior state (rather than it being 'about' this experience). The poem is 'requiring' mind-shapes to be or fit into *its* syntax, its page/shape momentarily. His images that arise (in the sense of the process of the poem sequence mirroring the process of meditation) are world and the person/Michael McClure ("INNER AND OUTER REALM MATED/IN SIZELESSNESS," "Plum Stone Two") *already there* but torqued by being language as if 'every thing as *one*'; yet shape is experienced/felt as a quiet half (as if 'every thing as one' is sliced in half vertically): it is non-image that allows inner and outer to be sensed as if both are *as* the same half.

W
I
N
T
E
R
in the shadow
thrown by a yellow violet

"Plum Stone Eight"

Imagined in order to be gauge of dimension, inner and outer, the 'two' (halves of space, or halves *in* space) can be melded, reorganized, and 'seen' only in poetry's language. The large (the category or realm of WINTER) is only seen as a shadow of its (here imagined) origin, *its* (WINTER's) "yellow violet." Thus changing conceptual proportion of space is the means of seeing into phenomena. The speaker, McClure, both inside and outside at once, in an earlier *and* a later time—and the reader having the sense of the 'half' of *all* as if vertically in sensorial space—implies an uncarved whole:

meat
conceived

of
it's

hunger

I
WAS
INSIDE
THE STREAM

listening to myself out there

BARGING AND CRASHING
IN A FANTASY
OF BOMBS

and gases
and children
being
raped
in prisons

and silver tinsel
on christmas trees

How precious is this pearl
of exploded harmony

"Plum Stone Four"

To draw together elements of McClure's poetry by considering sequence in "Crisis Blossom," a sequence from *Rain Mirror* (1999): Crisis leading to conversion as the poem, the catalyst is energy, which, amazingly, is as vital in McClure's current poetry as it is in his works written in 1957. He has a radical spirit, as which experiencing of crisis ("THE DARKEST,/ DENSEST/core") implodes sequence: the death of one is part of, and interrupted by, one's own birth ("I am nobody./Nobody is very large/and/ powerful./Birth is certain/for anyone dead" ("grafting thirteen," *Rain Mirror*). The "I" as blasted at core by the outside, the outside is occurring at once *from* the "I" as merely single unit and also melting-ground, similar to the yellow violet that is *in* winter being the *origin* of winter. The outside is from the "I" and "*There* is/ZERO,/and the nonstructure of nada inside.// EVERY//THING//is//FULL//BLAST" ("flower," my italics). Everything both starts again and is occurring full blast at once. As characteristic of radical spirit, "reason" for McClure is not authority (is never authority-principle); it is not merely social as 'sanity' or will (such as, 'the reason made or given for doing something, the reason given for bombing Iraq'). Rather, it is faculty—the individual's faculty—but also the faculty *in phenomena*. "THE SUBSTRATE IS SO VIBRANT/that I can't get close to it. It is YOU. YOU who are/*as* the owl hoots" ("grafting fourteen," my italics). The phenomenal substrate (in the latter passage) is the beloved person (YOU) existing *as* (and as *in*) the instant.

His formal rendition in a poem pairs the individual person and the large context (of universe, of society) as if language reflects 'mystery of being' *in that separation* (separation of language from one; and separation of one from macrocosm). Seeing the particular instance, in the outside, reveals or is the appearance of the rules that both govern the individual and at once manifest *in* them: "THE CLOUD THAT RAPHAEL FOUND is the rules of freedom" ("grafting seventeen"). Yet for the reader this is a state of awareness actually possible created only in the language that's the poem. We're alert in reading, centered. There is no *actual* relation between the *structure* of the biological organism and language; his language is his imagination and choice as that is also a manifestation of the body politic.

For example, "Poisoned Wheat," McClure's poem opposing the U.S. war in Vietnam, declaring the people at present to be separate from (to be guiltless of) the present or past actions of violent governing is a seeing 'the people free to alter the present.' As such freedom, we do not have fixed nature.

Selections from long sequences are included in *Of Indigo and Saffron,* also selections (from *Fragments of Perseus,* only two poems; from *September Blackberries,* three poems) from books composed of discrete poems so perfectly balanced in their ordering '*as book*' as to comprise structure of sequence difficult or impossible to render (to represent) other than *as* the book. In McClure's sequences, there is a sense of ontogeny recapitulating phylogeny: which (definition) is, stages (of the individual fetus) go through the process—*have* mirrored *in* its future—the evolution of the whole past and future (species) without the future of the species being known, not yet unfolding (or formed). McClure's forms as seeming to see them/selves (see one's forms) convey future in the present. At the same time all parts of design seem to reproduce each other but are unplanned, in the sense of unknown before (are discovered). As the statement of politics in "Poisoned Wheat," "there must be a milieu for action."

The chronological order of McClure's books is retained in *Of Indigo and Saffron,* with two exceptions: one of these is that I wanted to begin with seven poems from the fourteen-poem sequence "Organism" (written for the "On Organism" topic in Charles Olson's series "The Curriculum of the Soul," 1974) as my sense of that poem offering an introduction by *demonstrating* aspects of McClure's poetry (its propositions of being's enactment as language-form's action). The poems of the first edition of "Organism" (each printed on one large page) could be folded in the middle; the lines of the second half of all of the poems are duplicated exactly by the lines of the first half as if the mind/shape 'there' is replicating 'itself' yet both sides the same and also expanded differently; as if a butterfly's wing repeating its other side is its mirror image, the lines as statements of diaphanous detail appear to be producing a universe. The sound or rhythm of his repetitions in "Organism" take on an exhilarating speed (in reading the entire sequence); a rhythm, as if producing phenomena, can be heard in the *sound* in lines, or in the actual repetitions of lines in *other* poems showing up later in *Of Indigo and Saffron.* As such, the form he creates is as if mind-shape and universe duplicating each other: "The instant is the giant lamp we throw/ our shadows by" ("Ode," in *Star*).

McClure described (in conversation) his intention or basis in *Swirls in Asphalt,* the new poem sequence that concludes *Of Indigo and Saffron*: each particle (or poem in the sequence) is an instant (the reader undeviating from attention in this instant), and all parts are the same instant. To this reader the poem as infinite instant that is also apparently movement of the present comes across as the act of a most profound love poem: seemingly proportionlessness is throughout simplicity in utter openness: the borderless centered lines incorporating all objects and events—and being seemingly a span of time *as perceiving* these at once. The only light struggle as such is physical—awareness—as almost effortless act of reading in which the attention of the reader is held throughout.

The gesture of *Swirls in Asphalt* goes past the use of 'barrier' or 'blockage as enactment,' the form of conflict that was apparent in earlier poems.

Swirls in Asphalt is not based in duality of the self's separation, of language's separation from phenomena as the means of its apprehension: "'BLIND SEEING'/surrounds/the divine,/BREAKS THE KNOT" ("12 ['BLIND SEEING']"). Recalling the passage from "Crisis Blossom" ("THE SUB-STRATE IS SO VIBRANT/that I can't get close to it. It is YOU. YOU who are/as the owl hoots")—in *Swirls in Asphalt*, "YOU" (addressing Amy, also implicitly the readers) are the vibrant substrate and are "as" the owl hoots: are at the same time (and as brief) as the owl hoots, as is *in time* a being subject to dying yet *being* (vibrantly) transience. The same instant everywhere is time that "does not come and go" ("39 [TRANSIENCY LIKE THE SHAPE]," referencing Zen Master Dōgen), and is also the time-*being* (since the nature of time is that it *appears* to come and go), a horizontal and all-over space akin to a waterfall. "BLIND SEEING" is one's '*envisioning*' (mind's eye in which one sees both past and future), or apprehension that is outside of optical seeing yet *contains the details of optical seeing* (as if 'already,' overall) and renders these. As that same instant (that's the lines of text) the sense of motion that is the poem appears to hurl forward. *Swirls in Asphalt* is a seemingly endless same-time *phenomenal* instigation, as if the individual perceiver's instigation and that of all levels and dimensions broadly. Consciousness and imagination are coming from all parts of the outward flow (the text)—yet the instant of attention reading the poem is as if a waterfall '*now*' only, being the midst of action.

NOTES

1. Richard Candida Smith, *Utopia and Dissent: Art, Poetry, and Politics in California* (Berkeley: University of California Press, 1995), 339.

2. Interview with Harald Mesch, in Michael McClure, *Lighting the Corners: On Art, Nature, and the Visionary, Essays and Interviews* (Albuquerque: University of New Mexico Press, 1993), 10.

3. Robert Creeley, "For Michael," in "A Symposium on McClure," ed. John Jacob, special issue, *Margins* 18 (1975).

4. Smith, *Utopia and Dissent*, 336. My italics.

5. McClure, *Lighting the Corners*, 9.

6. Interview with Jack Foley, in *Beat Scene* 40 (March/April 2002): 17.

7. "Michael McClure: January 26, 1966," *USA: Poetry*, NET Outtake Series. VHS. KQED, 1966.

8. McClure, *Lighting the Corners*, 12.

SEVEN POEMS FROM *On Organism,* 1974

I

EACH BON MOT HAS COST ME A PURSE OF GOLD.
ERASE THE LINES OF THE NIGHT FROM THE COUCH OF THE
DAY.
COOL TURQUOISE CRYSTAL FEATHER — WOLF PROTON GYRE.
SCROLLED FERN SHADOW SPORE — BREAST SALT MOON.
Wheel of the galaxy turning in tumbleweed.
Faces of antelope staring from ice cream.
Watches ticking on the backs of turtles.
Tambourines tinkling in apple trees.
Flames full of creatures arising from the mouths of worms.
Bearded men pondering in dreams.
Bees and moths darting on the fields of purple asters.
Odor of hummingbird mint crunched under boot heel.
Maya.
Spirit.
Matter.
River.
Creek.
River.
Matter.
Spirit.
Maya.
Odor of hummingbird mint crunched under boot heel.
Bees and moths darting on the fields of purple asters.
Bearded men pondering in dreams.

Flames full of creatures arising from the mouths of worms.

Tambourines tinkling in apple trees.

Watches ticking on the backs of turtles.

Faces of antelope staring from ice cream.

Wheel of the galaxy turning in tumbleweed.

SCROLLED FERN SHADOW SPORE — BREAST SALT MOON.

COOL TURQUOISE CRYSTAL FEATHER — WOLF PROTON GYRE.

ERASE THE LINES OF THE NIGHT FROM THE COUCH OF THE
DAY.

EACH BON MOT HAS COST ME A PURSE OF GOLD.

A PROTEIN MOLECULE IS AN ELECTROMAGNETIC
SCULPTURE CHANGING IN TIME.
POETS ARE THE UNACKNOWLEDGED LEGISLATORS OF THE
WORLD.
BROW VAIN POLLEN DOLLAR — ROAR FOG SHIT.
VELVET TARTAN CURSE — MILDEW BERRY THUNDER.
White spined bushes on the mountainside caught at sunrise and moondown.
Swift lizards with blue throats rushing past stink beetles.
Music of children singing lost words.
Tails of donkeys hung on walls of a cavern.
Honey flowing over polished marble in fluorescent light.
Catatonic tables spouting fountains of nectar.
Vast deserts of kindness in a ball of cotton.
Gentle fingers touching neck muscles in pain.
Orion.
Taurus.
Pleiades.
Web of liquid galaxies.
Pleiades.
Taurus.
Orion.
Gentle fingers touching neck muscles in pain.
Vast deserts of kindness in a ball of cotton.
Catatonic tables spouting fountains of nectar.
Honey flowing over polished marble in fluorescent light.
Tails of donkeys hung on walls of a cavern.
Music of children singing lost words.
Swift lizards with blue throats rushing past stink beetles.
White spined bushes on the mountainside caught at sunrise and moondown.
VELVET TARTAN CURSE — MILDEW BERRY THUNDER.
BROW VAIN POLLEN DOLLAR — ROAR FOG SHIT.
POETS ARE THE UNACKNOWLEDGED LEGISLATORS OF THE
WORLD.
A PROTEIN MOLECULE IS AN ELECTROMAGNETIC
SCULPTURE CHANGING IN TIME.

I AM A PARCEL OF VAIN STRIVINGS TIED
BY A CHANCE BOND TOGETHER.
CLOVE PLASTIC SNEER POLLEN MESSIAH FEATHER.
ROSE MORNING LONE BREAD HUNGER.
Helmet and armor streaked with sun in the dark room.
Glitter of morning on rows of rectangular windows.
Naked woman in boots masturbating a horse.
Scream of a dying rabbit.
Breath of a baby on mirrors.
Nasturtiums lying on delicate lace.
Ivory rings set with sapphires.
Smell of black coal in the thicket of junipers.
Holes in quasars.
Aminos.
Rain drops.
Assez eu!
Rain drops.
Aminos.
Holes in quasars.
Smell of black coal in the thicket of junipers.
Ivory rings set with sapphires.
Nasturtiums lying on delicate lace.
Breath of a baby on mirrors.
Scream of a dying rabbit.
Naked woman in boots masturbating a horse.
Glitter of morning on rows of rectangular windows.
Helmet and armor streaked with sun in the dark room.
ROSE MORNING LONE BREAD HUNGER.
CLOVE PLASTIC SNEER POLLEN MESSIAH FEATHER.
I AM A PARCEL OF VAIN STRIVINGS TIED
BY A CHANCE BOND TOGETHER.

4

THE WORLD OF REASON IS TO BE REGARDED AS A GREAT AND
IMMORTAL BEING, WHO CEASELESSLY WORKS OUT WHAT
IS NECESSARY,
AND SO MAKES HIMSELF LORD ALSO OVER WHAT IS
ACCIDENTAL.
REVIVE THE PLEISTOCENE!
CURSE MUSK LICHEN SCARF BEARDED RAIN.
FLASHING RHYME TENTACLE SALMON HEART.
Bulky creatures eating the tops of lilac trees.
Peaks in the smog covered with fragile vines.
New spices exploding in the cups of tongue-beings.
Basalt boulders covered with ecru silk.
A yellow feather with a black bar.
Projections of reflected light from the eye-shields of owls.
A gray kitten biting the puppy's stomach.
Dainty wings on the man's head.
Rainbow.
Curves of dots.
Slender line.
Opal.
Slender line.
Curves of dots.
Rainbow.
Dainty wings on the man's head.
A gray kitten biting the puppy's stomach.
Projections of reflected light from the eye-shields of owls.
A yellow feather with a black bar.
Basalt boulders covered with ecru silk.
New spices exploding in the cups of tongue-beings.
Peaks in the smog covered with fragile vines.
Bulky creatures eating the tops of lilac trees.
FLASHING RHYME TENTACLE SALMON HEART.
CURSE MUSK LICHEN SCARF BEARDED RAIN.
REVIVE THE PLEISTOCENE!

THE WORLD OF REASON IS TO BE REGARDED AS A GREAT AND
IMMORTAL BEING, WHO CEASELESSLY WORKS OUT WHAT
IS NECESSARY,
AND SO MAKES HIMSELF LORD ALSO OVER WHAT IS
ACCIDENTAL.

6

CUPID ONCE DID NOT SEE A BEE SLEEPING AMONG ROSES.
THE SATELLITE SURROUND IS THE NEW ARTISTIC MASK WORN
BY THE EARTH ITSELF.
HUG SUGAR NOSTRIL WINE.
GYRE CELL PAVEMENT STREAMING MEMORY.
Merry crackle of orange flames in the black pit.
Pine cones hurtling through eternity.
Gingerbread men and scent of cardamom.
The old hen running with the worm.
The octopus burned at the stake.
Thick cream mixed with honey and apricots.
Toy sailboat in the flooding gutter.
An ancient millipede coiled and sleeping.
Grains of serpentine.
Cilia.
Hazelnuts.
Tuft.
Hazelnuts.
Cilia.
Grains of serpentine.
An ancient millipede coiled and sleeping.
Toy sailboat in the flooding gutter.
Thick cream mixed with honey and apricots.
The octopus burned at the stake.
The old hen running with the worm.
Gingerbread men and scent of cardamom.
Pine cones hurtling through eternity.
Merry crackle of orange flames in the black pit.
GYRE CELL PAVEMENT STREAMING MEMORY.
HUG SUGAR NOSTRIL WINE.
THE SATELLITE SURROUND IS THE NEW ARTISTIC MASK WORN
BY THE EARTH ITSELF.
CUPID ONCE DID NOT SEE A BEE SLEEPING AMONG ROSES.
THOR   THOR

8

NIRVANA ALSO DEPENDS ON THE TREASURES OF THE
TATHAGATA.
YET DEATH IS NEVER A WHOLLY WELCOME GUEST.
SWIM MUSIC BARK GLOAMING THUNDER.
LISTENING SMOKE SHEET WRINKLE MORNING.
A blackened face with clouds of blue smoke from the forehead.
Russian wolfhound crunching the ribs of sheep.
An envelope filled with orchid seeds.
Bright green creatures.
Appearance of the Ghost of Love.
Chairs covered with moss.
Palm trees the size of bacteria.
The sexual thrill of darkened autos.
Ammonia.
Ammonites.
Pineapple.
Silver dollars in the stocking.
Pineapple.
Ammonites.
Ammonia.
The sexual thrill of darkened autos.
Palm trees the size of bacteria.
Chairs covered with moss.
Appearance of the Ghost of Love.
Bright green creatures.
An envelope filled with orchid seeds.
Russian wolfhound crunching the ribs of sheep.
A blackened face with clouds of blue smoke from the forehead.
LISTENING SMOKE SHEET WRINKLE MORNING.
SWIM MUSIC BARK GLOAMING THUNDER.
YET DEATH IS NEVER A WHOLLY WELCOME GUEST.
NIRVANA ALSO DEPENDS ON THE TREASURES OF THE
TATHAGATA.

9

THE TOTAL AMOUNT OF GENETIC MATERIAL
IN CELLS PROBABLY INCREASED THEN, AS IT IS KNOWN
TO DO TODAY (IN PART AT LEAST) BY GENETIC
DUPLICATIONS.

THE SCIENCE OF THE SUFIS AIMS AT DETACHING
THE HEART FROM ALL THAT IS NOT GOD, AND AT GIVING
TO IT FOR SOLE OCCUPATION THE MEDITATION OF THE
DIVINE BEING.

TENTACLE CLAW FEATHER SHIT MEAT ROAR.

TRACERY WOLF ROSE HUNGER PRAISE.

Cyclones spinning over glaciers.

Confetti lying on empty beaches.

Antelope skull among ferns.

Children dancing on a cliff in the sunset.

A black dog shitting.

Mouthprint on the window.

Tiny insects carrying pollen.

Skyscraper snapping in the earthquake.

Odor of birds.

Eyebrows.

Fossilized shark tooth.

Rusty fur.

Fossilized shark tooth.

Eyebrows.

Odor of birds.

Skyscraper snapping in the earthquake.

Tiny insects carrying pollen.

Mouthprint on the window.

A black dog shitting.

Children dancing on a cliff in the sunset.

Antelope skull among ferns.

Confetti lying on empty beaches.

Cyclones spinning over glaciers.

TRACERY WOLF ROSE HUNGER PRAISE.

TENTACLE CLAW FEATHER SHIT MEAT ROAR.

THE SCIENCE OF THE SUFIS AIMS AT DETACHING THE HEART FROM ALL THAT IS NOT GOD, AND AT GIVING TO IT FOR SOLE OCCUPATION THE MEDITATION OF THE DIVINE BEING.

THE TOTAL AMOUNT OF GENETIC MATERIAL IN CELLS PROBABLY INCREASED THEN, AS IT IS KNOWN TO DO TODAY (IN PART AT LEAST) BY GENETIC DUPLICATIONS.

Of Indigo and Saffron

FROM *HYMNS TO ST. GERYON,*
1959

The Breech

A barricade — a wall — a stronghold,
Sinister and joyous, of indigo and saffron —
To hurl myself against!
To crush or
To be a part of the wall . . .
Spattered brains or the imprint
of a violent foot —
To crumble loose some brilliant masonry
Or knock it down —
To send pieces flying
Like stars!

To be the chalice of the hunt,
To handspring
Through a barrier of white trees!

At work — 3:00 in the morning — In the produce market
Moving crates of lettuce and cauliflower — Predawn
A vision — the rats become chinchillas — I stand
At the base of cliff — sweating — flaming — in terror and joy
Surrounded in the mist — by whirling circles of dark
Chattering animals — a black lynx stares from the hole
In the cliff.

Rotten lettuce — perfume — The damp carroty street.

It is my head — These are my hands.
I don't will it.

Out in the light — Noon — the City.
A Wall — a stronghold.

Poem

Linked part to part, toe to knee, eye to thumb
Motile, feral, a blockhouse of sweat
The smell of the hunt's
A stench, . . . my foetor.
The eye a bridegroom of torture
Colors are linked by spirit
Euglena, giraffe, frog
Creatures of grace — Rishi
Of their own right.

As I walk my legs say to me 'Run
There is joy in swiftness'
As I speak my tongue says to me 'Sing
There is joy in thought,
The size of the word
Is its own flight from crabbedness.'

And the leaf is an ache
And love an ache in the back.
The stone a creature.

A PALISADE

The inside whitewashed.

```
.   .   .   .   .   .
.   .   .   .   .  .
.   .   .   .  .
.   .   .   .   !
```

A pale tuft of grass.

Point Lobos: Animism

It is possible my friend,
If I have a fat belly
That the wolf lives on fat
Gnawing slowly
Through a visceral night of rancor.
It is possible that the absence of pain
May be so great
That the possibility of care
May be impossible.

Perhaps to know pain.
Anxiety, rather than the fear
Of the fear of anxiety.
This talk of miracles!

Of Animism:
I have been in a spot so full of spirits
That even the most joyful animist
Brooded
When all in sight was less to be cared about
Than death
And there was no noise in the ears
That mattered.
(I knelt in the shade
By a cold salt pool
And felt the entrance of hate
On many legs,
The soul like a clambering
Water vascular system.

No scuttling could matter
Yet I formed in my mind
The most beautiful
Of maxims.
How could I care
For your illness or mine?)
This talk of bodies!

It is impossible to speak
Of lupine or tulips
When one may read
His name
Spelled by the mold on the stumps
When the forest moves about one.

Heel. Nostril.
Light. Light! Light!
This is the bird's song
You may tell it
To your children.

For the Death of 100 Whales

... Killer whales ... Savage sea cannibals up to 30 feet long with teeth like
bayonets ... one was caught with 14 seals and 13 porpoises in its belly ...
often tear at boats and nets ... destroyed thousands of dollars worth of fishing
tackle ... Icelandic government appealed to the U.S., which has thousands
of men stationed at a lonely NATO airbase on the subarctic island.
Seventy-nine bored G.I.'s responded with enthusiasm. Armed with rifles
and machine guns one posse of Americans climbed into four small boats and
in one morning wiped out a pack of 100 killers ...
... First the killers were rounded up into a tight formation with
concentrated machine gun fire, then moved out again one by one, for the final
blast which would kill them ... as one was wounded, the others would set
upon it and tear it to pieces with their jagged teeth ...
TIME, APRIL 1954

Hung midsea
Like a boat mid-air
The Liners boiled their pastures:
The Liners of flesh,
The Arctic steamers.

Brains the size of a football
Mouths the size of a door.

The sleek wolves
Mowers and reapers of sea kine.
THE GIANT TADPOLES
(Meat their algae)
Lept
Like sheep or children.
Shot from the sea's bore.
Turned and twisted
(Goya!!)
Flung blood and sperm.
Incense.
Gnashed at their tails and brothers,
Cursed Christ of mammals,

Snapped at the sun,
Ran for the sea's floor.

Goya! Goya!
Oh Lawrence
No angels dance those bridges.
OH GUN! OH BOW!
There are no churches in the waves,
No holiness,
No passages or crossings
From the beasts' wet shore.

.

Poem

I wanted to turn to electricity — I needed
a catalyst to turn to pure fire.
We lied
to each other. Promises

are lies. Work is death. Contracts are
filth — the act of keeping them
destroys the desire to hold them.

I forgive you. Free me!

The Mystery of the Hunt

It's the mystery of the hunt that intrigues me,
That drives us like lemmings, but cautiously —
The search for a bright square cloud — the scent of lemon verbena —
Or to learn rules for the game the sea otters
Play in the surf.

It is these small things — and the secret behind them
That fill the heart.
The pattern, the spirit, the fiery demon
That link them together
And pull their freedom into our senses,

The smell of a shrub, a cloud, the action of animals

— The rising, the exuberance, when the mystery is unveiled.
It is these small things

That when brought into vision become an inferno.

Peyote Poem

Clear — the senses bright — sitting in the black chair — Rocker —
the white walls reflecting the color of clouds
moving over the sun. Intimacies! The rooms

not important — but like divisions of all space
of all hideousness and beauty. I hear
the music of myself and write it down

for no one to read. I pass fantasies as they
sing to me with Circe-Voices. I visit
among the peoples of myself and know all
I need to know.

I KNOW EVERYTHING! I PASS INTO THE ROOM

there is a golden bed radiating all light

the air is full of silver hangings and sheathes

I smile to myself. I know

all that there is to know. I see all there

is to feel. I am friendly with the ache
in my belly. The answer

to love is my voice. There is no Time!
No answers. The answer to feeling is my feeling.

The answer to joy is joy without feeling.

The room is a multicolored cherub
of air and bright colors. The pain in my stomach
is warm and tender. I am smiling. The pain
is many pointed, without anguish.

Light changes the room from yellows to violet!

The dark brown space behind the door is precious
intimate, silent and still. The birthplace
of Brahms. I know

all that I need to know. There is no hurry.

I read the meanings of scratched walls and cracked ceilings.

I am separate. I close my eyes in divinity and pain.

I blink in solemnity and unsolemn joy.

I smile at myself in my movements. Walking
I step higher in carefulness. I fill

space with myself. I see the secret and distinct
patterns of smoke from my mouth

I am without care part of all. Distinct.
I am separate from gloom and beauty. I see all.

(SPACIOUSNESS

And grim intensity — close within myself. No longer
a cloud
but flesh real as rock. Like Herakles
of primordial substance and vitality.
And not even afraid of the thing shorn of glamor

but accepting.
The beautiful things are not of ourselves

but I watch them. Among them.

And the Indian thing. It is true!
Here in my Apartment I think tribal thoughts.)

STOMACHE!!!

There is no time. I am visited by a man
who is the god of foxes

there is dirt under the nails of his paw
fresh from his den.
We smile at one another in recognition.

I am free from Time. I accept it without triumph

— a fact.

Closing my eyes there are flashes of light.

My eyes won't focus but leap. I see that I have three feet.
I see seven places at once!
The floor slants — the room slopes
things melt
into each other. Flashes
of light
and meldings. I wait

seeing the physical thing pass.

I am on a mesa of time and space.

¡STOM-ACHE!

Writing the music of life
in words.
Hearing the round sounds of the guitar
as colors.
Feeling the touch of flesh.

Seeing the loose chaos of words
on the page.
(ultimate grace)
(Sweet Yeats and his ball of hashish.)

———————————————————

My belly and I are two individuals
joined together
in life.

THIS IS THE POWERFUL KNOWLEDGE
we smile with it.

At the window I look into the blue-gray
gloom of dreariness.
I am warm. Into the dragon of space.
I stare into clouds seeing
their misty convolutions.
The whirls of vapor

I will small clouds out of existence.

They become fish devouring each other.

And change like Dante's holy spirits

becoming an osprey frozen skyhigh

to challenge me.

2

The huge bird with bug eyes. Caught in dynamic profile.
Feet stretched out forward
glaring at me.
Feathery cloudtips of feathers
dark gray on gray against blue.

From the cliff of the park — the city — a twilight
foggy vista. Green grass over the stone,
pink auras of neon. The spires lean

into the clouds. I remember the window, wonder.

Out over the rooftops from the window.

I am at the top of the park. I look

for the clouds in the calm sky.

Tendrils and wisps. I see 180 degrees.

MY STOMACH IS SWOLLEN AND NUMB!

I have entered the essential-barrenness
there is no beauty the exotic has come to an end I face the facts
of emptiness, I recognize that time is a measurement is arbitrary,
I look for the glamor of metamorphosis, for the color of transmutation,
I wait to become the flask of a wonder to see diamonds, there is no
purpose. Pain without anguish space without loveliness. The pure
facts of vision are here there is the City! There is the wonder
as far as the eye can see the close buildings I see them so close.
Oh and I am so glad to see them. This is the change

that I do not care but know.

THE GIANT, COMIC, FIERCE, BIRD FROM MY WINDOW!

The spirits, souls rising to form it need no explanation
in the world.
Vast expanse without interest — undrab.

Here is the light full of grains and color
the pink auras and flesh orange. The rasping sounds,

hideous buildings leaning into emptiness.

The fact of my division is simple I am a spirit
of flesh in the cold air. I need no answer

I do not lean on others. I am separate, distinct.

There is nothing to drag me down.

Back at the window again I look for the Osprey

I remember the flow of blood, the heat
and the cold almost-fear beneath it. There is nothing

in the night but fast clouds. No stars. Smokey gray
and black the rooms are the color of blue Mexican glass
and white. I see to the undercoats of paint

to the green and brown. I am caught in reveries of love.

The tassles of the shag rug are lace.

I am in the Park above all and cold.

I am in the room in light Hell and warm Heaven.

I am lost in memories. I move feeling the pleasant bulk
of my body. I am pleased with my warm pain

I think of its cessation with pleasure.

I know it will not change. I know I am here, beyond all

in myself.

The passage — my eyes ache with joy in the warmth.

The edge of the cloth like tassles — a shag rug

white — the loops lace over your shoulder —

the white wall behind — green showing through
lace again a sweet memory in the gloom.

The smells clear in my head over your shoulder.
Your brown arm on the tick cloth. Blue stripes

on white the smell of smoke and the smell of bodies.

Oh and the void again with space and no Time.
Our breath moving in the corners of the room!

3

I AM MOVING IN THE YELLOW KITCHEN
high never to come down — the ceiling brown.

I am looking at the face of the red clock —
meaningless.

I know of the sky from my window and I do not turn
to look, I am
motionless forever standing unmoving —
a body of flesh in the empty air.

I am in the barren warm universe of no Time.
The ache in my belly is a solid thing.
There is no joy or tremor, I smoke a cigarette in the small
room elbow to the stove seeing what is new —
barren as my cigarette and hand in the air hearing the whir of unheard
sounds, seeing the place of new things to the air. In
no relation, feeling the solid blankness of all things having

my stomach solid and aching, I am aloof
and we are one,
in the bare room my stomach and I held together by dry
warmth in space.
There is no reason for this! There is nothing but forms
in emptiness — unugly
and without beauty. It is that.

I AM STANDING HERE MYSELF BY THE STOVE
without reason or time.
I am the warmth and it is within me.

BELLY BELLY BELLY! UNENDING AND BLANK.

I am in the instant of space, I see all I am aware of all
I am curious but knowing that there is no more than this — the happenings

of the world continue about me there are whorls and wisps of smoke
there are the sounds of late afternoon and early evening
with forever between them I see it passing between them
I cannot be surprised — there is no news to me it has always been
this way — going into a memory would be to go into a long
black tunnel. The room is huge and spacious without
PATTERN OR REASON. IT HAS ALWAYS BEEN THIS WAY.
THERE ARE THE COLORS
of early evening as they have always been. I am as I shall
always be. Standing feeling myself in the inert.

I raise my head with the beauty of final knowledge
I step high in pride benevolence and awareness. The pain

is part of me. The pain in my belly. The clouds
are passing and I will not stop them.

COLOR IS REALITY! THE EYE IS A MATCHFLAME!

The pain is a solid lump — all of the anguish
I am freed from.

The answer to joy is joy without feeling. The answer to love

is my voice.

The room is a solid of objects and air.

I KNOW EVERYTHING, I AM FILLED WITH WEARINESS

I close my eyes in divinity and pain.

I blink in solemnity and unsolemn joy.

I am free of the instant there is no Time!

I have lived out the phases of life from patterned opulence
to stark and unheeding.

My stomach is gentle love, gentle love.

I AM AT THE POINT OF ALL HUGENESS AND MEANING

The pain of my stomach has entered my chest
throat and head.

The enormous leap! I look from the precipice

of my window.
I watch from my warmth, feeling.

THERE ARE NO CATEGORIES!!!

(OH WONDER, WONDER, IN DREARINESS AND BEAUTY
aloof in perpetual unamazed astonishment warm
as stone in the emptiness of vast space
seeing the small and limitless scale
of vastness. My hand before me. Seeing

all reachable and real. The answer to love
is my voice.
I am sure. This is the ultimate
about me. My feelings real to me. Solid

as walls. — I see the meaning
of walls — divisions of space,
backgrounds of color.)

HEAVEN AND HELL THIS IS REACHABLE I AM SICK IN LACK
OF JOY

and joyful in lack of joy and sick
in sickness of joy. Oh dry
stomach! And not ecstatic in knowledge.

I KNOW ALL THAT THERE IS TO KNOW,

feel all that there is to feel.

Piteously clear air. Radiance without glow.

Perfection.

I hear all that there is to hear.
There is no noise but a lack of sound.
I am on the plain of Space.

There are no spirits but spirits.

The room is empty of all but visible things.

THERE ARE NO CATEGORIES! OR JUSTIFICATIONS!

I am sure of my movements I am a bulk
in the air.

FROM *A FIST FULL*, 1956–1957

The Air

for Robert and Jess

Clumsy, astonished. Puzzled
as the gazelle cracked
in my forepaws/

The light body twitches/

A slight breeze moves among whiskers.

The air curves itself to song.
A trace, a scent lost among whiskers.
A form carved in the air
and lost by eye or ear.
The herd's thunder or the whack
of a tail on earth
evident only in dim vibration
less than a whirr of brush (and bushes).
Not a sound in a flat stone.
(Less than a fly
about the ears.)
An object, a voice, an odor.
A grain moving before the eyes.
A rising of gases/
An object/
An instant/ Tiny, brighter
than sunlight.

The sound of a herd. The sound of a rock/
A passing.

Two Weeks Baby Sunbathing

This old brown velvet
by daylight is not eternal velvet
but the baby on it, bright in the morning sun,
is more beautiful than human.
Her glory fills the room.
Her back and buttocks are mounds
of color.
Her toes and fingers are fat stars.
Light streams between the drapes
and, incandescent, she changes it
to orange, to pink, reflecting on the face
bent over her and gleaming from the leaves
of the houseplants.

Jane

For a Drawing by Jess

The horse—it's not a horse!—Phoenix!—
flashes up. His speed streams behind him
past the gray mesa
(Max Ernst in the shape of a goggle-eyed bird
stares in disbelief
at the passing)
—through the sonic barrier of slim clouds
and black stars.

His cock (arm? wing?) hangs limp
not realizing the speed of the passage
giving belief to the motion.

Into the fat clouds and pollywogs,
the whirlwind rushes from him.

On into the violent black rain!

FROM *DARK BROWN*, 1961

*the struggle to it is DARK BROWN the struggle
itself is a solid moving in an inferno . . .*

OH GIDDY BLANK WHITE PAGE OH DREAMY MAN OH
INTERRED SPIRIT BULK
in meat and hand. Oh both
are one! Oh love black white and dream Rose and Purple,
and green and scratched. Oh sleeping Lion,
man. Oh beast. Oh Black
ODEM. OH

Depth within. Oh limited void, as far
as eyes can see and nose can smell. Oh dreamer.
OH PRIDE GOD SHIT AND ACHING STRETCH RIB. NO NOT

Lion not the shit of metaphor. The deep and
singing beast! Void instead! OH

---

crap upon the page.

I dream and walk in my dream with proud stride. I am clean
and dream with brown eye. I am free
OF LIBERTY.

THE BODY THE SPIRIT ARE ONE I AM
energy!

" am muscled space. Am meat
and colored light.
ROMANTIC CRY

THE ROOT THE ION THE PRIDE TO THE LEAF THE BLOOD
AND ORGANS
to the Beast. OH BLOOD OH CRY SHIT GOD CHRIST

THE SHOUT AND SLAM OF FOOT IN THE HOLLOW ROOM

THE WINDING OF MUSIC WITHIN IT

Not music but the sound of what is felt. Sound
made by the interior. (The words are small
I fail.) The Romantic cry
and structure. Blake's invention. The
SOUND the TORCH
in the dark cave, this last note.
The thing made and heard by the beast, the pride
of the flower. The pride of the ion?
That this is all a whole in a greater space
and matters more. And goes on

NO! I RELENT TO EASE

A last final failure again. My triumph.
The pride of my shape. The pride of my love. The pride
of myself. The pride of my child. The pride
of my pride. The pride of my loud foot typing hands and
hair. That I
broaden that I will not give surcease
save that I rest that my motions will be
stronger.   !

THE GREAT LONG DAMNED AND UNDAMNING /thing/
PATH

THE CLOUDLESS CLEAR AND BLACK

((OH BRING OH BLOOD BACK THE COURAGE THE DEEP THE
NEGATIVE CHALLENGE
I deny. Love. Deny. Defy oh love. In blackness
a forest, oh damp earth. Put forth. Decry! Put down
until a shoot is sent forth matching. The purity
the image within. Oh crass and easy polemic

say:
! I LOVE !
Let me be a torch to myself.))
OH HEART-SICK BURN STRIVE Past the drift-ease
to the depth within making a film of the gene
over the surface. *Say* meat hand, the hand black
in the deed as the strain toward the act. Each strike
an ugly huge music. Walking walking huge Love.

All a web from the black gene to the black
edge.
(((torture destroy tradition seek what gives damned
pleasure.)))
Exult in drugs
draw back to sight,
VISION

of purity & liberty.
MORTALITY IS BEAUTY THE BEAST SPIRIT LIVES FOREVER
!   !

!

I REST

OH WHY OH WHY THE BLASTED LOVE THE HUGE SHAPE
CHANGE? OH WHY
the tortured hand when clouds are down? I love
your lips and hands and legs. Your backbone line,
your breasts. The movement of your face and move
from them now. Oh why the words of lies above. Oh why the shape
change of movement, energy? when I will return to you
Oh awkward Love awkward, I love your
fingertips. Oh black
and sorrowed night. Oh mother and child.
Must I learn new love anew. No
choice! Are we joined forever
or is that lies! I remember
love in darkness and feel of flesh. Oh
CHANGE

No ease to truth. I half admit it.

OH EASE OH BODY-STRAIN OH LOVE OH EASE ME NOT!
WOUND-BORE
be real, show organs, show blood, OH let me
be as a flower. Let ugliness arise without care
grow side by side with beauty. Oh twist
be real to me. Fly smoke! Meat-real, as nerves
TENDON
Ion, FLAME, Muscle, not banners but bulks as
we are all 'deer'
and move as beasts. Stalking in our forest
as these are speech-words!

Burn them pure as above they rise from attitude are
stultified. Are shit. Burn
what arises from habit. Let custom
die. Smash patterns and forms let spirit
free to blasting liberty. Smash the
habit shit above!!!!!!!!!

LET PURE BLACK WORDS MOVE FROM THOUGHT BEHIND

ABAVED DEARN A-DEARN DEATH-FEAR WHY Are you here?

OH BRIGHT MAN WHY FLAME-FEAR WHEN YOU ARE BLACK
and dive into blackness. Into the swart
dark-brownness and now live in fires. Apitch

tuned and sent rushing, impeded
tossed back, channeled, rifted, serried
TEDIUM
I mean become a stream rushing, branches
waving. Sent in fear. Regretting. Tossed
by anothers face and
hand. Why
OH GOD FUCK SWEET BREATH RUSHING SHIT DO I

REPEAT LOVE REPEAT?
Confused by the confusion. I Beast
am star. Am same as star. Call on sweet-
ness to be not sweet. Enroil what I contain
in the tube of me. Breathe. Pneumas.
Call of oh stark. I
STRETCH RAISE RISE PUT FORTH AS

AN IRIS. MY BLOOD MY BREATH

DEEP-DELVE

refuse fuck to sing. Oh. OH.

Hate the silly fucking image.

PROFANE, PROFANE.

(((TO YOUR HUGE SMOOTH FACE AND HAND, BODY,
SMOOTH, IN

warm touch evening cool. I strike sick longing,
forgiving you. Wanting forgiveness. To lost
in the small words. Lost in the untensile
HEARING ANOTHER VOICE LOVE YOU
/LOSE YOU/
Lost love the outline of my body. Lose sight
in pictures of the love I have. Oh else!
I COME! ((AWAY-DREAMING.))
And all that too incorporated. Held

IN THE BODY LIKE A NERVE
geryon, a false beauty, fraud

HOW TO PUT IT DOWN? HOW TO CEASE??

Cease!

OH SMOKE-MAKING INTENT DREAMING OF ELSEWHERE
sick lip-service to a small shrieking voice.
Do you love me oh? As I love you?)))

FROM *THE NEW BOOK/A BOOK OF TORTURE*, 1961

Ode to Jackson Pollock

Hand swinging the loops of paint — splashes — drips —
chic lavender, *duende* black, blue and red!

Jackson Pollock my sorrow is selfish. I won't meet
you here. I see your crossings of paint!
We are all lost in the cloud of our gestures —

— the smoke we make with our arms. I cry
to my beloved too. We are lost
in lovelessness. Our sorrows
before us. Copy them in air! We
make their postures with our stance.

They grow before us.
The lean black she-wolves on altars of color.
We search our remembrance for memories
of heroic anguish. We put down
our pain as singing testimony.
Gouges, corruptions, wrinkles, held loose

in the net of our feelings and hues —
we crash into their machinery making it
as we believe. I say

we. I — You. You saw the brightness
of pain. Ambition. We give in to the lie
of beauty in the step of creating.
Make lies to live in. I mean you. Held
yourself in animal suffering.
You made your history. Of Pain.

Making it real for beauty, for ambition
and power. Invented totems from teacups
and cigarettes. Put it all down
in disbelief — waiting — forcing.
Each gesture painting. — Caught on
to the method of making each motion
your speech, your love, your rack

and found yourself. Heroic — huge — burning
with your feelings. Like making money
makes the body move. Calls you to action
swirling the paint and studying the feeling

caught up in the struggle and leading it.
For the beauty of animal action
and freedom of full reward.
To see it down — and praise — and admiration,
to lead, to feel yourself above all others.

NO MATTER WHAT — IT'S THERE! NO ONE

can remove it. Done in full power.
Liberty and Jackson Pollock the creator.
The mind is given credit.

You strangled
the lean wolf beloved to yourself —
Guardians of the Secret
— and found yourself the secret
spread in clouds of color

burning yourself and falling like rain

transmuted into grace and glory, free
of innocence

containing all, pressing experience
through yourself onto the canvas.
Pollock I know you are there! Pollock
do you hear me? !! Spoke to himself
beloved. As I speak to myself
to Pollock into the air. And fall short

of the body of the beloved hovering
always before him. Her face
not a fact, memory or experience
but there in the air
destroying confidence.
The enormous figure of her mystery

always there in trappings of reason.

Worked at his sureness. Demanding
Her place beside him. Called

from the whirls of paint, asked for
a face and shoulders to stand naked
before him to make a star.

He pulling the torn parts of her body
together
to make a perfect figure — 1951.
Assembled the lovely shape of chaos.
Seeing it bare and hideous, new
to the old eye. Stark
black and white. The perfect figure
lying in it peering from it.
And he gave her what limbs and lovely face
he could
from the squares, angles, loops, splashes, broken shapes
he saw of all with bare eye and body.

The Chamber

for Jack Kerouac

IN LIGHT ROOM IN DARK HELL IN UMBER AND CHROME,
I sit feeling the swell of the cloud made about by movement

of arm leg and tongue. In reflections of gold
light. Tints and flashes of gold and amber spearing
and glinting. Blur glass . . . blue Glass,

black telephone. Matchflame of violet and flesh
seen in the clear bright light. It is not night

and night too. In Hell, there are stars outside.

And long sounds of cars. Brown shadows on walls
in the light
of the room. I sit or stand

wanting the huge reality of touch and love.
In the turned room. Remember the long-ago dream

of stuffed animals (owl, fox) in a dark shop. Wanting
only the purity of clean colors and new shapes
and feelings.
I WOULD CRY FOR THEM USELESSLY

I have ten years left to worship youth
Billy the Kid, Rimbaud, Jean Harlow
IN DARK HELL IN LIGHT ROOM IN UMBER AND CHROME I
feel the swell of
smoke the drain and flow of motion of exhaustion, the long sounds of cars
the brown shadows
on the wall. I sit or stand. Caught in the net of glints from corner table to
dull plane
from knob to floor, angles of flat light, daggers of beams. Staring at love's face.
The telephone in cataleptic light. Matchflames of blue and red seen in the
clear grain.
I see myself — ourselves — in Hell without radiance. Reflections that we are.

The long cars make sounds and brown shadows over the wall.

I am real as you are real whom I speak to.
I raise my head, see over the edge of my nose. Look up

and see that nothing is changed. There is no flash
to my eyes. No change to the room.

Vita Nuova — No! The dead, dead, world.
The strain of desire is only a heroic gesture.
An agony to be so in pain without release

when love is a word or kiss.

Ode for Soft Voice

And sometimes in the cool night I see you are an animal
LIKE NO OTHER AND HAVE AS STRANGE A SCENT AS ANY
AND MY BREATH
energy go out to you.
And see love as an invention and play it extemporaneously.

And I who cannot love can love you.
OH THIS THIS THIS IS THE HURT / THAT WE DO NOT KICK
down the walls and do not see them.
And I do not ache until I scent you. And I
do not scent you. Breathing moves us. Breath is . . .

And more than this that we are huge and clear
and open — locked inside
and moving out and we make outlines in the air the shapes
they are. And we shift so. We move and never keep our forms but stare
at them address them as if they were there. This is my hand with
5 fingers, my heart nerves lungs
are there and part of me
and I move.
I have no form but lies and drop them from me.

I am a shape and meet you
at our skins' edge.
We change and speak and make our histories. I am all I feel
and what you see and what you touch.
There are no walls but ones we make.
I AM SICK CONFUSED AND DROP IT FROM ME
The nerves are dead that feel no hunger or pain there's no triumph
but failure. This is the last speech of seraphim or beast sick in need for
change and chaos. The room of banished love for beauty. The tooth in
our breast. What we see is real and able to our hand, what we feel is
beauty (BEAUTY) what we strike is hatred, what we scent is odorous.
This about me is my bride if I kick aside the forms of it for woman world
and mineral for air for earth for fire and water for table chair and blood.

Yes Table

YES AND HANDS AND ARMS YES TABLE DARK SQUATTY
AND STRONG
at night I lie in pain and sorrow,
in shadow I am a seraphim — miserable and sick

my dreams are not memories,
so much is blotted out that I am only here.
So much to remember, so much to remember, so much to remember.
This is a war. The instant's
history.
(In the night I awoke and remembered you and you were gone

though you lay by my side. I searched for you among the silver

hangings, I could not speak your name. I wandered in the long hall.)
etc.

From *For Artaud*

for Wallace Berman

AND ALL HUGE AND ALL/

I am a flask sealed and nothing is happening!
I am black and I do not move out. See
nothing. Or for an instant I am tall look down
on all as it is fit
for seeing. That all is water clear and running,
solid and wavering,
that all is real and I walk in it. Among it.

And see in a face or breast an animal
loveliness.
And feel my chest and stomach beat for it.

AND IT IS NOT LOVELINESS! BUT CLARITY BUT PURE
responding. When I see
a breast I love. Or face of suffering.
In the cold water black worms (planarians)
move and dart or crawl unseen.
And all is clear holy and not beautiful
to them.
But icy light icy dark and green wet leaves
above.

La Plus Blanche

JEAN HARLOW, YOU ARE IN BEAUTY ON DARK EARTH
WITH WHITE FEET! MICHAEL
slaying the dragon is not more wonderful than you. To air
you give magical sleekness. We shall carry you into Space
on our shoulders. You triumph over all with warm legs and a
smile of wistful anxiety that's cover for the honesty
spoken by your grace! Inner energy presses out to you in warmness —

You return love. Love returned for admiration! Strangeness
is returned by you for desire. How. Where
but in the depth of Jean Harlow is such strangeness
made into grace? How many women are more beautiful
in shape and apparition! How few can / have /

draw such love to them? For you are the whole creature of love!

Your muscles are love muscles!

Your nerves — Love nerves!

And your upturned
comic eyes!
Sleep dreams of you.

Rant Block

for Jay DeFeo

THERE IS NO FORM BUT SHAPE! NO LOGIC BUT SEQUENCE!
SHAPE the cloak and being of love, desire, hatred,
hunger. BULK or BODY OF WHAT WE ARE AND STRIVE
FOR. ((OR
there is a series of synaptic
stars. Lines of them. It's that simple
or brutal. And, worst, they
become blurred.

SNOUT EYES
As negative as beauty is.))
LEVIATHAN WE SWOOP DOWN AND COVER
what is ours. Desires
OR BLOCK THEM. SICKNESS — ACHES.
Are heroes in simplicity with open eyes
and hungers. Truth
does not hurt us. Is more difficult than
beauty is. We smolder smoke pours
from our ears in stopping what we feel.
(free air)
Your hand, by your side, is never love.

FORUM IS AN EVASION! POETRY
A PATTERN TO BE FILLED BY FAGGOTS.

WILD ANGER MORE THAN CULTIVATED LOVE!!
Wolf and salmon shapes free to kill
for food love and hatred.
Life twists its head *from side to side* to test
the elements and seek
for breath and meat to feed on.
I AM A FIRE AND I MOVE IN AN INFERNO
sick I smolder
and do not burn clear.

Smoldering makes nets of smoke upon the world.
I am clean free and radiant and beauty follows this.
Not first but follows.
What is love or hatred but a voice I hear
of what I see and touch. Who is the man
within that moves me that I never see
but hear and speak to? Who are you
to stop me? Why are you here
to block me? All I choose to see
is beauty. Nerves. Inferno!
Fakery of emotions. Desire for presumption. Love of glory. Pride.
Vanity. Dead and unfilled desires. Regrets. Tired arms. Tables. Lies.
BLOOD AND MUSCLE BLOOD AND MUSCLE BLOOD
AND MUSCLE BLOOD AND MUSCLE
Calling pure love lust to block myself and die with that upon my head?
Wit and false stupidity with no point to it but the most tangled ends
unwitnessed by myself in fulfillment. When I found you sleeping
why didn't I? Would you love me for it? Do I care? OH. And smoke.
AND NOT THAT FINE SWING
of wing or fin!

And never chivalry. The strive to rise. The act of grace. Of self.
Of sureness large enough for generosity. The overflowing.
But the chiding carping voice and action. What is this? Why
DON'T WE KICK IN THE WALLS? KICK IN THE WALLS!
INVENT OURSELVES IN IMAGES OF WHAT WE FEEL.

WHERE HAVE ALL THESE CLOUDS OF SMOKE COME FROM?
I am the animal seraph that I know I am!

And I burn with fine pure love and fire, electricity and oxygen
a thing of protein and desire, !!
and all of this is ugliness and talk not freedom
OH SHIT HELL FUCK THAT WE ARE BLOCKED
in striving by what we hate
surrounding us. And do not break it in our strike
at it. The part of us

so trained to live in filth and never stir.
THAT I WAIT FOR YOU TO RAISE YOUR HAND FIRST
(to me)
This is sickness. This is what
I hate within
myself. This
is the war I battle in. This is the neverending instant.
The black hour that never ceases. This is the darkness about
the burning.
The form and talk of form as if flames obeyed without
dwindling.

These are the dull words from an animal of real flesh. Why?
Where is the fire in them?
Never let them stop until they are
moving things. Until
they stir the fire!
Never let them stand stemmed by form again. Let
my face be radiant and give off light!
Never allow sign of love where hatred dwells!

If there are bastions, let my love be walls!

FROM *LITTLE ODES,* 1961

Ode

The Love and VISION of the Instant are the venom we coil
our tiny bodies on. I am this sensual!
I AM THIS SIZE!! I AM THIS SIZE
AND THERE IS NO OTHER AS WE LIE COILED
in the black lily of our lives.
The instant is the giant lamp we throw
our shadows by. I love you honeyed venom.
The instant is without thorn and I cannot be
hung on it
the instant is not rose but lily
and we may be fairy creatures
HUGER THAN THE STARS!!!

BREAK DOWN THE STINKING SWEAT OF FEAR
that rises in my nose like flames!

NOT THE UGLY PLAIN SPEECH AMONG THE REAL SCULPTURES
OF THE REAL
HELL AND UGLINESS but the soft warmth of eternal imagination
and delicate beauty. Rise to me from your blossom instant
make new capitals and smash the old. Ignore the falsity
and

Ode

OH BLACK AND COLD I SEE IN // AND DRAW UTTER GRACE
FROM YOU

NOW I SEE ONLY THE FEAR AND AGONY!!!

MY MUSCLES ARE MY EXACT SPIRIT, the sight of my Soul
I believe no more. My soul appeared
to say that I am a child and will die a child
to appear no more. That I had lived
but once before — as a killer whale — and
that I shall dive in blackness
free of the chain of meat

& the joy is gone!!!
I want to drink the purple wine
of Shadows

NO! NO! NO! NO! NO! NO! NO! NO! NO!
I DEMAND THE BLACKNESS! THE BLACKNESS! THE BLACKNESS!!
BLACK BLACK BLACK BLACKNESS BLACKNESS BLACKNESS BLACK
BLACK BLACK BLACKNESS! MY PLACE AT THE BLACK TABLE
IN BLACKNESS! MY BLACK PLACE AT THE BLACK
TABLE OF BLACKNESS TO DRINK AND EAT BLACKNESS
IN THE BLACKNESS AT THE GREAT
TABLE OF NEVER!!!!!

in the blackness
and my face painted forever by Raphael!

Hummingbird Ode

THE FAR-DARTER IS DEAD IN MY HAND, THE BEAUTIFUL
SHABBY COLORS!!
and the damp spots where the eyes were. Small form
that was all spirit, smashed on the plate
glass window. The green head and ruby
ruffles. The beautiful shabby colors
and the damp spots where the eyes were.
All head and chest and the Eros-spear
of the beak. Moving like Cupid
in the fuschias.
Hummingbird and spike of desire.

The huge chest and head and the beautiful
shabby colors. Tiny legs
thrust back in the last stiff agony.

WHAT'S
ON YOUR SIDE OF THE VEIL??
DO YOU DIP YOUR BEAK
in the vast black lily
of space? Does the sweetness
of the pain go on forever?

IS THERE COURAGE THERE IN THE NIGHT?
WHERE ARE THE LOVES THAT MAKE THE BLOSSOM
of your body? Do they still spin
in the air? Your wives
and loves? Are you now
more than this meat? Finally
A STAR??

Ode

MY WORDS ARE PLAIN, GIVE GRACE, CONTAIN NOBILITY.
THE MEAT
of man is the speech of his spirit. Speech
is the thinnest meat of man — but physical!
In the plainness is grace that leads me
through to sight of vibrant
spiritmen and spiritladies, that dance

and stride in their grace and make their bestial
stampings in romantic warmth on cold
reality. I love the eye
of love and the tender hand. I cast
myself before them like a rose. Pluck
me, my tears are dew. And flesh
trembles at the sight
of you. THE FINGER OF LOVE
IS DELICATE AND THE VOICE
IS COARSE

ONLY YOUR BODY CAN SPEAK WITH WORDS
only your love can be a finger.

THIS IS MY EMPTINESS AND COMIC DANCE
warm, warm by the fire. Speak!

SCRATCH OUT THE SHIT OF TRADITION — OF DANCE
and comedy

Fantasy Ode

WITHIN, I HAVE FELT REVOLT AND RIPPED MYSELF FROM MYSELF.
I FEEL REVOLT AND RIP MYSELF, til my
eyes spread and my nostrils burn, becoming the infant

of myself's desires. AND THE DESIRES WERE STOPPED, SMASHED
by myself. AND ONLY THE BURNING IS REAL.
Til I grasp with my physical body (the size of my spirit)
and shake myself from myself.

And the desires are stopped, smashed!!

And I move in the deep pool of the black Lily
of Space. Like a worm without Head
dashing in the rich cool pollen
and blackness, mindlessly scenting the perfumes
and feeling the flesh of the petals
on my belly and senses.

AND O, I AM LOST O, IN THE LILY
without eyes
and
HUNGRY! !AND REAL

In each man's meat are many individuals but only
one SELF and it must conquer and lead to health
and the natural body-physiology!

Ode

WILDNESSES AND HIGH ACT LIE IN A FABRIC THAT YOU
ARE WEAVING!!
You are most sure of beating
blood, and warmth of your creation.

QUICK, LIVELY, you act before sight lands on the slow sight.
YOU SAY YOU ARE A JEWEL NOT A FLOWER! I wear the desire
of your changing being.

YOU OF DARK FREE SENSORY AWARENESS AND INFANT
SIMPLICITY,

what trails of beauty and Spirit.
AT NIGHT, SLEEP BECOMES WHITE AWE AND WONDER.

FROM *GHOST TANTRAS*, 1964

1

GOOOOOOR! GOOOOOOOOOOR!
GOOOOOOOOOR!
GRAHHH! GRAHH! GRAHH!
Grah gooooor! Ghahh! Graaarr! Greeeeer! Grayowhr!
Greeeeee
GRAHHRR! RAHHR! GRAGHHRR! RAHR!
RAHR! RAHHR! GRAHHHR! GAHHR! HRAHR!
BE NOT SUGAR BUT BE LOVE
looking for sugar!
GAHHHHHHHH!
ROWRR!
GROOOOOOOOOOH!

2

PLEASURE FEARS ME, FOOT ROSE, FOOT BREATH,
BY BLAHHR MOKGROOOOOOO TARRR
nowp tytath brooooooooooooooooooooo

———

In the middle of the night I dreamed I was a creature
like the great Tibetan Yogi Milarepa.
I sang a song beginning:
"Home lies in front of you not in the past.
Follow your nose
to it."
It had great mystic import, both apparent and hidden.
I was pleased with it.
GOOOOOOOOOOR!
GROOOOOOOOOOOOOOOOOOOOH!
GOOOOOOOO.
ROOOOOOOOOOOH!
POWFF! RAHH! BLAHHR!

OH LOVELY LINE BETWEEN DAY AND DREAM.
We slip over and under thee
when we are pleased and richly placid.
REFUGE FOR ALL SENTIENT BEINGS!
WHO ART THOU, I, ME?
HOOOOOOO! HOOOOOO! GRAHH!
GROOOOOOOOOH! GROOOOOH! NAHHR
MHEE!
RRGAHH!
Grooor Kayve.
MWAHH!
Greeeeeeeeee-groooooo.
GARHRRROOOOOOOOOOOOOOH
WHOOG KLOWBB.
(What is not sentient? But I — more than all —
am a whole full universe.)
FULL. MAKE GROOOOR.

MARILYN MONROE, TODAY THOU HAST PASSED
THE DARK BARRIER
— diving in a swirl of golden hair.
I hope you have entered a sacred paradise for full
warm bodies, full lips, full hips, and laughing eyes!
AHH GHROOOR. ROOOHR. NOH THAT OHH!
OOOH...
Farewell perfect mammal.

Fare thee well from thy silken couch and dark day!
AHH GRHHROOOR! AHH ROOOOH. GARR
nah ooth eeze farewell. Moor droon fahra rahoor
rahoor, rahoor. Thee ahh-oh oh thahrr
noh grooh rahhr.

August 6, 1962

49

SILENCE THE EYES! BECALM THE SENSES!
Drive drooor from the fresh repugnance, thou whole,
thou feeling creature. Live not for others but affect thyself
from thy enhanced interior — believing what thou carry.
Thy trillionic multitude of grahh, vhooshes, and silences.
Oh you are heavier and dimmer than you knew
and more solid and full of pleasure.
Grahhr! Grahhhr! Ghrahhhrrr! Ghrahhr. Grahhrrr.
Grahhrr-grahhhhrr! Grahhr. Gahrahhrr Ghrahhhrrrr.
Ghrarrrr. Ghrahhr! Ghrarrrrr. Gharrrr. Ghrahhhrr.
Ghrahhrr. Ghrahr. Grahhr. Grahharrr. Grahhrr.
Grahhhhr. Grahhhr. Gahar. Ghrahhr. Grahhr. Grahhr.
Ghrahhr. Grahhhr. Grahhr. Gratharrr! Grahhr.
Ghrahrr. Ghraaaaaaahrr. Grhar. Ghhrarrr! Grahhrr.
Ghrahrr. Gharr! Ghrahhhhr. Grahhrr. Ghraherrr.

a reading with lions, San Francisco Zoo

I LOVE TO THINK OF THE RED PURPLE ROSE
IN THE DARKNESS COOLED BY THE NIGHT.
We are served by machines making satins
of sounds.
Each blot of sound is a bud or a stahr.
Body eats bouquets of the ear's vista.
Gahhhrrr boody eers noze eyes deem thou.
NOH. NAH-OHH
hrooor. VOOOR-NAH! GAHROOOOO ME.
Nah droooooh seerch. NAH THEE!
The machines are too dull when we
are lion-poems that move & breathe.
WHAN WE GROOOOOOOOOOOOOOOR
hann dree myketoth sharoo sreee thah noh deeeeeemed ez.
Whan eeeethoooze hrohh.

THE STARS ARE A SHIELD OF NOTHING
CREATED OF NOTHING
AND I CALL ON THEE TO SWING,
ashahh harr marrr gahrooo yahr aye-howw tanthor rahrr
ooohrnah thownie toww smeels tor sheen
thah gahreems wooven mah laughter eehn nroh
beyond the final first devi now shemetter
poor ahn gras nowerhoww hayrayoar
bleth tomakayne grahhr shageer
raise up thy heeze ahn streee entoh eeze.
LOOK UP!
See our calm, titanic, minuscule gestures.
YAHRR NOH. HRAHHHRR-NOHH!

IN TRANQUILITY THY GRAHRR AYOHH
ROOHOOERING
GRAHAYAOR GAHARRR GRAHHR GAHHR
THEOWSH NARR GAHROOOOOOOOH GAHRR
GRAH GAHRRR! GRAYHEEOARR GRAHRGM
THAHRR NEEOWSH DYE YEOR GAHRR
grah grooom gahhr nowrt thowtooom obleeomosh.
AHH THEEAHH! GAHR GRAH NAYEEROOOO
GAHROOOOOM GRHH GARAHHRR OH THY
NOOOSHEORRTOMESH GREEEEGRAHARRR
OH THOU HERE, HERE, HERE IN MY FLESH
RAISING THE CURTAIN
HAIEAYORR-REEEEHORRRR
in tranquility.

FROM *STAR*, 1970

Mad Sonnet

THE PLUMES OF LOVE ARE BLACK! THE PLUMES OF LOVE ARE
BLACK
AND DELICATE!   OH!
and shine like moron-eyed plumes of a peacock
with violetshine and yellow on shadowy black.
They spray SPRAY from the body of the Beloved. Vanes shaking in air!

AND I DO NOT WANT BLACK PLUMES OR AGONY ... AND I DO
NOT SURRENDER. And I ask for noble combat!!
to give pure Love
as best I can
with opened heart
LOVE!!
I have not seen you before and you're
more beautiful than a plume!

Stately, striding in Space and warm . . . (Your
human breasts!)
LET ME MAKE YOUR SMILE AND HEARTSHAPED FACE
IMMORTAL

YOUR GRAY EYES ARE WHAT I FINALLY COME TO WITH MY
BROWN!
AND YOUR HIGH CHEEKS, and your hair rough
for a woman's—like a lamb. And the walking Virtue
that you are!

Love Lion

OH FUCKING LOVER ROAR WITH JOY—I, LION MAN!

I GROAN, I AM, UPON THE CONE SHAPED BREASTS

& tossing thighs!

—AND SEND MY THOUGHTS INTO A BLACKER UNIVERSE
OF SUGAR!
Thy face is a strained sheer Heart twisted
to fine beauty by thy coming.

It is a million miles from toes to thighs!
(Our bodies beat like the ultimate movie
slowed to blurs of two meat clouds becoming
one—and the Undersoul is joined
by kissing mouths.)

OH!

OH!

And I am some simple cub
with plump muscles, loving immortality!

THE SHEETS ARE WHITE.

THE PILLOW SOFT.

JESUS HOW I HATE THE MIDDLE COURSE!

Thy Eyes! Thy Eyes!

Cold Saturday Mad Sonnet

for Allen Ginsberg

ON COLD SATURDAY I WALKED IN THE EMPTY VALLEY OF
WALL STREET.

I dreamed with the hanging concrete eagles
and I spoke with the black-bronze foot of Washington.
I strode in the vibrations
of money-strength
in the narrow, cold, lovely CHASM.

Oh perfect chill slot of space!

WALL STREET, WALL STREET,
MOUNTED WITH DEAD BEASTS AND MEN
and metal placards greened and darkened.
AND A CATHEDRAL AT YOUR HEAD!

I see that the men are alive and born
and inspired
by the moving beauty of their (own) physical figures
who will tear
the vibrations-of-strength from the vibrations-of-money
and drop them like a dollar on the chests
of the Senate!
They step with the pride of a continent.

Mad Sonnet 2

OH HOW I WANT THEE FAME!
FAME, THOU VIOLET LAOCOÖN OF TOILING BRAWN
and writhing snakes enwreathed on upturned
GRIEVED FACES.
Oil and sweat shake from the locks of the famous,
and though they moan they are stoic as a tree.
Fame loops out fat coils like a half-forgotten dream
and binds men's wrists in their romantic agony.

Fame, you are a rotten plum!
I wipe you from my fingers
with a rosy napkin.

- -

LET ME SEE THE LOVE TENDRILS
of woman and child!
AWAY FAME!

My spirit is not trapped by love of fame.

I am not hungry for death's attitudes.

BLESS NIGHT.

Poisoned Wheat

OH, BLUE GRAY GREEN PALE GRAHHR!
TRANQUIL POURING ROSE LION SALT!

There is death in Viet Nam!
There is death in Viet Nam!
There is death in Viet Nam!
And our bodies are mad with the forgotten
memory that we are creatures!

Blue-black skull rose lust boot!

Citizens of the United States
are in the hands of traitors
who ignore their will and force
them into silent acceptance
of needless and undesired warfare.

EACH MAN, WOMAN, CHILD
is innocent
and not responsible
for the atrocities committed by any
government. Mistakes, hypocrisies, crimes
that result in the present
FASCISM
are made in the past in
HISTORY.
Structural mechanisms of Society
create guilt in the individual.
((Now it is worst when man is at the edge,
he may be freed of his
carnivore past—and is on the verge
of becoming a singer and glorious creature
borne free through the universe.
Soon no lamb or man
may be eaten
save
with the smile of sacrifice!))

It is our nature to explore
that which is called Evil
by the haters of matter
and pleasure. But GUILT
is untenable! Guilt is not
inheritable. Acceptance of guilt
for a Capitalist heritage creates fear.

NO ONE IS CULPABLE FOR THESE CRIMES!
We are flowers capable of creating the seeds
and fruit of new liberty.
Like beautiful flowers the profits of Capitalist
society are the blossoming
of the agonized labor and starvation
of the world's masses.
THAT I AM A FLOWER DOES NOT MEAN
THAT I AM RESPONSIBLE
FOR THE AGONY OF THE ROOTS!
But, as a man, I am conscious of the agony,
labor, pain. And murders take place
for Society!

Acceptance of guilt for the acts of
entrepreneurs, capitalists and imperialists
smothers, tricks, and stupefies

the free creature! He will, is, driven
to fear, racism, and inaction!

If I forget, for a prolonged moment,
the mammal, sensory pleasure of which
I am capable
I must toil to override
the creeping guilt that destroys
me spiritually!

I AM NOT GUILTY!

I AM A LIVING CREATURE!

I AM NOT RESPONSIBLE FOR THE TRAITOROUS
FASCISM AND TOTALITARIANISM THAT SURROUND me!!!

((The definitions of *fascism* and *totalitarianism*
must be reviewed in light of the new media developed
by technology. The nature of the human
mammal is being remade and it is time for
redefinitions . . .))

I AM NOT RESPONSIBLE
FOR THOSE WHO HAVE CREATED
AND / OR CAPTURED the CONTROL DEVICES
OF THE SOCIETY THAT SURROUNDS ME!
I despise Society that creates
bundles of individual cruelties
and presses them en masse
against the helpless.

I AM INNOCENT! In my innocence I may act creatively
and *not* fulfill a pre-prescribed pattern
of guilt leading to escapism and cynicism.

COMMUNISM WILL NOT WORK!
Communism will not create food in quantities
necessary for man's survival.

CAPITALISM IS FAILURE!
It creates overpopulation, slavery,
and starvation.

Whether I be in Soviet Russia, Red China, or Imperialist
England or France, or Capitalist United States,
I am not responsible for the fascist
or totalitarian crimes
that are whitewashed
under the name *Modern History!*
I AM INNOCENT AND FREE!
I AM A MAMMAL!

I AM A WARM-BLOODED SENSORY CREATURE
CAPABLE OF LOVE AND HATE AND ACTION AND INACTION!

CAPABLE OF GUILT AND CAPABLE
OF SPEECH AND STRIVING!

—I am sickened by the thought
(and photographs)
of cruel and vicious executions
and tortures of Asian
and Algerian soldiers.

I AM SICKENED
by the oncoming MASS STARVATION
and the concomitant revolting degree
of overpopulation, and the accompanying
production of incredible numbers
of useless physical objects
whose raw materials demand
a destruction of those parts of nature
I have come to think of as beautiful!
—THOUGH I REJOICE IN THE FOREST
AND CAVES OF THE FUTURE!

BEING SICKENED IS A LUXURY
that I cannot afford without loss
of spirit, gradually
becoming irreparable! I am a man!
Sickness *and* guilt must be cast off!
Guilt is a luxury.
Being sickened is meaningless.
CAPITALISM AND COMMUNISM ARE A POLITICAL
CONFRONTATION!

I have escaped politics. I disavow
the meeting whether it is a means to
war or coexistence!
The meanings of Marxism and Laissez-faire
are extinct.

The population of the United States will double
by the year 2000. Certain South American
nations double each eighteen and twenty years.
There is no answer
but a multiplicity of answers created by men.
A large proportion of men are on the verge
OF STARVATION!
When density of creature to creature reaches
a certain degree
the ultra-crowded condition is a
biological sink.
Rats in overpopulation experiments
become insane in predictable types . . .
perverts, cannibals, hoods, criminals, and semi-
catatonics. When crowding reaches a certain
point the animals respond by more need
and desire
for crowding!
!SAN FRANCISCO, TOKYO, LONDON, MOSCOW, PEKING!

The human being is the commonest object!

Each human being must be responded to.
There are too many for the nervous system.
Man evolved as a social creature
and rare animal. He is now
the commonest large animal
—and threatens all other creatures with extinction.

((In the Neolithic, men made both plants and animals
subject to his appetites through cultivation
and domestication—the stress
of this guilt began a genetic change in his
being. He mutated himself—population
began.
Now he is capable of freeing himself
from the Neolithic Revolution

and must choose between
song and suicide!))

Cynicism and escapism are the shapes
of reaction to the torture and slaughter
of Asians, Asians placed
in overpopulation and starvation
by European and American imperialism . . .
By outright conquest and introduction
of technology into non-technological nations.
Colonial nations are directed to produce
products desired by the West.
They are trained as consumers
of Western material artifacts.
They are given Western medicine which lowers
the mortality rate.

If an American accepts these facts he must assume
guilt and responsibility!
THIS IS NOT SO! Society will have
the individual feel guilt so that he will fly
from the possibility of action.
SOCIETY WILL THEN PERPETUATE THE STATUS QUO OF
SOCIETY!

But this is not true for Society is insane.
A status quo is not being perpetuated.
Society is masochistic.
It deludes itself that a status quo is
maintained. It is driving for its destruction.
WESTERN SOCIETY HAS ALREADY DESTROYED ITSELF!
The Culture is extinct! The last sentry
at the gate has pressed the muzzle to his
forehead and pulled the trigger!
The new civilization will not be communism!
POLITICS ARE AS DEAD AS THE CULTURE
they supported!

Politics are theories regarding the speculated
laws of power—their applications
have never touched men except in shapes
of repression!
NEW SOCIETY WILL BE BIOLOGICAL!

HISTORY IS INVALID BECAUSE WE ARE ESCAPED
FROM HISTORY. As individuals we inhabit
a plateau where civilization is perpetuated
by the mechanisms of a rapidly dying and masochistic
Society. We are supported by traitors
and barbarians who operate war
utilizing the business principles of this Society.

THOSE WHO CAN SEE AND FEEL ARE IN HIDING THEY HOPE
for a few years of life before the holocaust.
They are caught up in the forms of evangelism
that are hysterical reaction
to population density. They hope
for a miracle. The thrill of the beauty
of the new music and entertainment media—as well
as religion—are evangelism.
It is beautiful that even hysteria can be made
to give assurance and pleasure and some means
of satisfaction
—BUT IT IS A LAST DITCH BIOLOGICAL REACTION

The small hope for salvation by means of utilization
of hysteria is pathetic!!!!!

The bombing of Asian fishing villages can be equated
to the new music / / save that one is beautiful
and one is not. The witness of the new intellectuals
testifies to the beauty of both!

Beauty IS hideous!
Mussolini spoke of the beauty of bombing
villages as the SS cherished the pleasure

of executing Jews! ((What INSANITY
to have Israel as thorn to the Arabs!))

The human mammal is not capable of receiving pleasure
from the tortured deaths of his own kind
without previous acceptance of insanity
or the development of insanity
within himself!
The masses of planes that fly over

ARE NOT PASSENGER SHIPS
but are bombers flying to Asia!

STOP UP THE EARS—it is true!

AND WHO IS FLYING THEM?

What name for those who accept authority
and enter the cockpits?
No doubt as in the bombing of Guernica!

What name for the voice of authority that tells
the pilots to enter the ships?

THE ACCEPTANCE OF THE IMPOSSIBLE IS CYNICISM!
To admire or be silent about pain and death
IS CYNICISM!
To enact a role when Society is a corpse
IS CYNICISM!

Whether the corpse be a young Soviet or Chinese or an old
U.S. corpse!

WITHDRAWAL FROM INFORMATION IS ESCAPISM!
Escape from the ears that hear the bombers pass?
Evangelism—whether it be of art or religion
is escapism.
There must be a milieu for action.
Barbarism,
Atrocities,
Bombings,

Poisonings
of wheat in Cambodia,
Secret Government agencies,

---

and all manifestations of political hysteria

LEAD TO GENOCIDE! OR MASS STARVATION
and such Hell that death would be better!

FREEDOM FROM GUILT AND RESPONSIBILITY
is necessary to the individual so he may
receive the normal pleasures of body and life
—whether it be the pleasures of a Congo tribesman
or a city dweller in a European or American city!

IDEALISM IS EASY FOR THE MOST WEALTHY AND THE MOST
IMPOVERISHED!

POLITICS IS DEAD AND BIOLOGY IS HERE!

FEAR AND GUILT MUST BE CAST ASIDE LIKE A DIRTY ROBE!

CYNICISM AND ESCAPISM MUST BE PUT ASIDE INSTANTLY!

The traitors directing the barbarism must have power taken
from them!

There is no single answer to the new biological confrontation!
There must be a multitude of solutions!
They must be arrived at by thought and action.
Neither is possible without energy and information!

Society and Government smother both energy and information!

The majority of the citizens are against the war!
War creates guilt that causes blindness!

Blindness means hysteria and flight!

An arena must be cleared for new thought and action
that is not national in scope
but incorporates all human creatures . . .

and all creatures to come!
—All who will move to the stars to investigate
the possibilities of infinite freedoms.

EACH MAN IS INNOCENT!
The point of life is not rest but action.
DEATH IS REST
—everyone will have enough rest for eternity!

NOW IS THE TIME FOR ACTION.
THE WAR MUST BE STOPPED—THE WORLD SEEN CLEARLY!

THE UNIVERSE IS MESSIAH!

WHAT IS THIS SMOKE?

The neon napalm flash is filth and death!

GRAHH!   BLESS!

FROM *HAIL THEE WHO PLAY,*
1974

for Jim Morrison

OH MUSE,

SING THAT I BE ME, BE THOU,

BE MEAT,

be me, be I, no ruse
—A MAMMALED MAN,
and stand
with rainbow robes
that drop away and globes
that float in air about my hand.
A UNIVERSE IN FIGURE EIGHTS
swirls about my head
in flashing neon-lighted dots and blurs and spots
and heavy lines of triumph energy
that lie within my skin.
I raise this knife, this wand, with blade
so thin . . .
I lie upon a circled, polished table
AND LEAP UP
to be myself again!!!!!

!OH POTENCY!
To be my self-soiled soul,

SPIRIT AGAIN,

AND NOTHING MORE!

I AM MY ABSTRACT ALCHEMIST OF FLESH
made real!
I AM MY ABSTRACT ALCHEMIST OF FLESH
made real!
I AM MY ABSTRACT ALCHEMIST OF FLESH
made real!
And nothing more!
NO LESS THAN STAR—
a chamber and a vacuole.
Without sense!   A Thing!   I feel!

I am not gold nor steel!
I am not metal, sulfur, nor the flow of Mercury!!!!
I am not the berry crumbling in my cheek
with rasping seeds that speak
of summer sun, or salmon in the creek
that stretch themselves, writhing
on the pebbled beach to catch the gasp of twilight
IN THE CAVERN OF THEIR MIGHT

and feel the sunbeam crash the slime

AND CATCH THE GLINT.

I'M SHEERLY ARM AND LEG
that bounces from the slashing beam
of heat
AND NOTHING MORE!!!!!!
!OH MUSE!
!OH ME!

FROM *SEPTEMBER BLACKBERRIES*, 1974

Written above the Sierras
in the Flyleaf of Regis Debray's
Revolution in the Revolution

for Joanna

Shouldst thou die, I'll be with thee
in the mountains of eternity
and fight thy cause with gun and harp.
I am only paws
and claws within this mortal world.
The map
of silk and marble
BOW TO THEE.
I praise FUTURITY
within the forests
of the mind
MADE REAL.

Running. Breathing. Speaking.

Beating music with a feather.

Gray Fox at Solstice

Waves crash and fluff jewel sand
in blackness. Ten feet from his den
the gray fox shits on the cliff edge
enjoying the beat of starlight
on his brow, and ocean
on his eardrums. The yearling
deer watches — trembling.
The fox's garden trails
down the precipice:
ice plant, wild strawberries,
succulents.
Squid eggs
in jelly bags (with moving
embryos) wash up on
the strand.
It is the night of the solstice.
The fox coughs,
"Hahh!"
Kicks his feet —
stretches.
Beautiful claw toes
in purple brodiaea lilies.
He dance-runs through
the Indian paintbrush.
Galaxies in spirals.
Galaxies in balls.
Near stars and white mist swirling.

Springs

1. I REMIND MYSELF THAT THE UNIVERSE I HAVE INHERITED IS DIVINE.
2. FACES DIVINE AND TWISTED.
3. STILL DIVINE.
4. VOICES SNEERING AND ARROGANT.
5. STILL DIVINE.
6. DISSOLVING CITIES — DIVINE.
7. FOX SPARROW, JUNCO, CANNIBAL SALAMANDER UNDER THE LEAVES — DIVINE.
8. PRESENCES OF ALL EXTINCT CREATURES — DIVINE.
9. THE ONE BODY OF ALL — OF WHICH I AM A FACE OR FINGER — DIVINE.
10. THE HEAD OF A WOLF PRESSES OUTWARD FROM THE ENDOPLASMIC RETICULUM OF A PHAGOCYTE, AND HOWLS AND SINGS.
11. A RAINBOW GLISTENS OVER THE SINGING WOLF HEAD.
12. DARK SHAPE-CREATURES FLOAT — MOVING — OVER THE RAINBOW.
13. SILVER GALAXIES FORM OVER THE SHAPE-CREATURES.
14. THE GALAXIES DRAW TOGETHER TO CREATE A PHAGOCYTE.
15. PINK PLUM PETALS FALL TO THE TABLE TOP.
16. LEAVES CURL DAY BY DAY.
17. SHAPE-CREATURES APPEAR IN THE VASE.
18. A BLUE VELVET NOTEBOOK AGAINST SLICK YELLOW CARDBOARD.
19. NOVALIS FLYING THROUGH SPACE WITH MADAME CURIE.
20. THE MYSTERY OF PORCHES AND DOORWAYS.
21. THE BLACK PERCEPTIONS OF CHILDHOOD DRAWING INTO A BALL IN THE OLD MAN.
22. FEARS CHANGED INTO LOVES — LOVES CHANGED INTO FEARS.
23. PIANOS — EXPLOSIVES — CAVERNS OF CRYSTAL.
24. MY DEAD FATHER WITH THE SMILE OF HIS BABY PICTURES.

25. EXHAUSTS OF AUTOMOBILES — DRAGON VAPORS FROM HOLES IN STEEL PLATES IN THE STREET.
26. DREAMS OF BABIES CREATING UNIVERSES.
27. THE ERODED BANK FALLING BACK INTO THE SALT MARSH.
28. PANDAS CHEWING BAMBOO SHOOTS IN CHINA.
29. THE UNKNOWN SUBSTITUTE FOR THE LUMINIFEROUS ETHER.
30. SHADOWS IN THE DESERT.
31. SHADE IN THE FOREST.
32. THE ODORS OF VENICE.
33. THE HARBOR OF HONG KONG — CHICKEN SHIT AND PERFUMES.
34. THE PLEASURE OF TRUTH.
35. THE FREE CONSTELLATIVE PATTERNS OF THE BODY.
36. CAVES OF BROKEN CONCRETE.
37. NEW MOSS.
38. THE CUPS OF LICHENS — A POOL FOR THE CONJUNCTION OF ALGAE AND FUNGI.
39. WARM SUNLIGHT — SWALLOWS SINGING BEFORE DAWN.
40. THE AGONY OF EXISTENCE IS DIVINE — SO IS THE PLEASURE.
41. WATERFALLS OF SOFT FUR.
42. SPRINGS OF COLORS INTERMIXING IN THE MEADOW.

Poetics

YES! THERE IS BUT ONE
POLITICS AND THAT
IS BIOLOGY.
BIOLOGY
IS
POLITICS.
We dive into
the black, black rainbow
of the end
unless we spend
our life and build love
in creation of
what is organic.
The old views
(worn and blasted)
are a structure
of death.
Our breath
IS
TO
SERVE
THE
ULTIMATE
beauty
of ourselves.

STANZAS FROM *RARE ANGEL*,
1975

LOVELINESS
OF GOLD FLAKES
SCATTERED INTO ERMINE.

.

OR
AM I A DEMON
with my head thrown
back and mouthing
words from this cave
of faces? Or am I
AN ANGEL
(all sweet and bright)
(warm, solid, real)
with arms crossed
and hands on biceps?

The poem that I'm writing is like a museum of living nudibranchs (a long line of clown messiahs) describing TOLTEC-ME and baby-me—and the way the surface of the Earth is an energy explosion that removes the Pleistocene and leaves only cinders in the shapes of bookends, rugs, and tractors. And even that (sadly) is a part of my "spiritual" development. So the poem has to rise by making a swooping swing so that the whole is finally (perhaps) a sublime perception locked into itself and reaching out. It is numberless trials that make a conscious and unconscious feedback loop.

A
PALACE FOR LARGE BLACK ANTS
at the base of the walnut tree.

Flick of swords slashing brows.

Flashlight beams playing over concrete.

My imagination
(only)
reaches warmth
across

the space.
Who knows what she sees.
The huge hairy animals haul themselves
along the plain and stop and eat
the bushes. By the water hole
men leap up out of silence
swinging clubs and screaming.
The hairy creatures stand in wonder
and terror and faintest
flicker of admiration for the painted faces . . .

∎

SO NOW IT'S SERIOUS,

YOU SAY.

You say it is serious.

You say it pours into itself
like honey poured from cup to cup.

THINGS ARE WHAT THEY ARE:
WAVES OF STARS OR DOTS.

I
KNOW
ALL
THAT!

The net of constellations
is as serious
(or laughable)
as I am.

THE

SILHOUETTE

OF

A

PELICAN

DIVING

BEAK

FIRST

into

WAVES.

Red and gray and blue
reflections flickered back and forth.

Dead friends speaking to me.

Sailing ship mirrored in its own wake.

SAND DOLLARS.

GIANT CACTI.

Huge rivers bursting through the mountains.

■

ANOTHER SPOT— SOMEWHERE
ELSE IN ANOTHER
SWIRL OF SPACE
or
untouchable
dimension
and I am writ upon it in modes of senses
that I do not comprehend.
It's here beneath my foot
or lost behind
another Milky Way.
The fire burns caverns in a cardboard box.
Black edges curl inward in red flames . . .

The sound of surf makes grottos
in my mind. Sand beneath
my elbow. Boulders of silicon
and serpentine and smooth crushed shell.
The helicopter is a bar of ruthless sound
across it all. The fall

TAKES
THE PRISONER
looping thirty thousand feet
with hands bound behind his back
while crowds of feasting gods
are singing his goodbye.
The jay turns over a brass button.

THE MONSTER OPENS HIS BLUNT FACE—EYES WIDE!
Snags of fur blow around his snout
in the savannah wind. Dragonflies
dart away from the water hole. The coppery
horsehair snakes move blindly—and indifferent—
frightening mosquito larvae with the clouds
of sediment. Waterstriders move back
among the cattails. The beast screams wheezingly
with fear and alarm. He raises one clawed
arm—half-turns—shit pours
from him into the pond.
One man rips him open
with the flint.
Blood pours like a little waterfall
from a fur mountain.

THEY YELL WITH GLEE
distorting stripes
of ochre and green
upon their faces.

The baby raven listens from his nest
on a nearby cliff.
Vultures think about it overhead.

Two things grow together in the darkness.

■

LOVE AND HUNGER COMPRISE HATRED.
HATRED AND LOVE
join to be hunger. Hatred and hunger are love.
It is a verbal exercise to show
that we
are made
in subtler ways
than our Platonic statements.
Everything
all melted down
and glossy-glassy
becomes an ethic like a green
plastic Parthenon
and

it

WILL

NEVER BEAT

OLD AGE OR DEATH!

No vacuum cleaner or opinion brings escape
or Liberation.

NO GURU
OR
MOSES
BRINGS
you

any
news
but your own winged smile!

— — — — — — — — — — — — — — — — — —

WE ARE AS FREE
as
everything
around
us!
Candles burning in the twilight.

Trucks growling in the dawn.

Floors rippling in an earthquake.

Embroidery upon the lips of clouds.

Thunderstorm above a cornfield.

Scent of pink silk and encyclopedias.

∎

DÜRER, RAPHAEL, AND SHANG DYNASTY
CRAFTSMAN OF BRONZE.
All are concerned with babes, madonnas,
tigers, owls.
They are
hypnotized by
(in love with)
gorgeous
shapes
of moiling intricacy
—and show them flat
or in faint relief.

They leave the eye to move around
in the material mind.

Let the neuron eye-light
flow around
the body of
a sun bear.
Let the eye-light
charge
in no known form
through
no
known blackness.
Let the blackness be indigo and melt in silver.
OUT
OF
IT
COMES THE SHADOW
OF MY FACE
OR YOURS.
It gains dimension
—then becomes a cliff with firs
—then a planetoid.
Now it is a psychic submarine and dives
streaming into
everywhere.
Then it becomes a hand to write with white music
in the shadows.
Cars carve the freeway up with sounds.

When we lose ourselves it is death, and Luck enters.
REBORN!

Brown hills flow gently towards
the mud flats.
Seals face the sunset.

Limpets under boards.

The antlered worms are artisans of hunger.

FROM *FRAGMENTS OF PERSEUS,*
1983

Dream: The Night of December 23rd

for Jane

—ALL HUGE LIKE GIANT FLIGHTLESS KIWIS TWICE THE
SIZE OF OSTRICHES,
they turned and walked away from us
and you were there Jane and you were twenty-two
but this was the nineteen-forties,
in Wichita, near the edge of town, in a field
surrounded by a copse of cottonwoods. It was
getting dark and the trees around the bridge
almost glowed like a scene by Palmer.
The two Giant Birds—Aepyorni—from Madagascar,
extincted A.D. one thousand, turned and walked
from us across the bridge. Even in the semi-darkness
the softness of their brown feathers made
curls pliant as a young mother's hair. There
was a sweet submission in the power of their enormous
legs (giant drumsticks). Their tiny heads
(in proportion to their bodies) were bent
utterly submerged in their business and sweeping
side to side as a salmon does—or as a wolf does—
but with a Pleistocene, self-involved gentleness
beyond our ken. My heart rose in my chest
(as the metaphysical poets say "with
purple wings of joy.") to see them back
in life again. We both looked, holding hands,
and I felt your wide-eyed drinking-in

of things.
Then I turned and viewed across the darkening
field and there was a huge flightless hunting fowl
(the kind that ate mammals in the Pliocene).
He stood on one leg in the setting sun by the sparkling
stream that cut across the meadow to the bridge.

He had a hammer head and curled beak, and after my
initial surge of fear to see the field was dotted,
populated, by his brethren, each standing in the setting

sun, I saw their stately nobility

and again

the self-involvement.

We followed the Aepyorni

across the old wooden bridge made of huge
timbers. The bridge was dark from the shadows
of the poplars and the evergreens there.
The stream was dimpled with flashing moonlight

—and I think it had a little song.

Then

I found that on the bridge we were among
a herd of black Wildebeests—Black Gnus.
One was two feet away—turned toward me—
looking me eye-into-eye. There was primal
wildness in the upstanding coarse (not
sleek as it really is in Africa) fur on
the knobby, powerful-like-buffalo shoulders.
(Remember this is a dream.) I passed by him
both afraid and unafraid of wildness as I had passed
through the herd of zebras at the top of Ngorongoro Crater
in front of the lodge, where from the cliff we could see
a herd of elephants like ants, and the soda lake
looked pink because of flamingos there.
There is an essence in fear overcome
and I overcame fright in passing by those zebras

and this black Wildebeest.

Then we passed

over the heavy bridge and down a little trail
on the far side of the meadow, walking back

in the direction we had been.

Soon we came

to a cottage of white clapboards
behind a big white clapboard house and knocked
on the door; it was answered by a young man
with long hair who was from the Incredible String Band.
He took us inside and he played an instrument
like a guitar and he danced as he played it.
The lyre-guitar was covered with square plastic
buttons in rows of given sizes and shapes.
The instrument would make any sound, play
any blues, make any creature sound, play
any melody . . . I wanted it
badly—it was a joy. My chest rose.
I figured I'd have to, and would be glad to,
give twenty or thirty thousand for it . . .
Then the dream broke
and I was standing somewhere with Joanna
to the side of a crowd of people by a wall
of masonry and I reached into my mouth
and took from my jaw (all the other
persons vanished and I was the center of everything)
a piece which was eight teeth
fused together. I stared at them
wondering how they could all be one piece.
They were white . . . It was some new fossil.
Down on the bone there were indentations like rivulets
like the flowing pattern of little rivers.

Captives

WHAT A PIECE OF BLACK
SPIRIT YOU ARE,

you who come
through the door

with a sleek
long tail

and yellow eyes
to sit

on my knees
as I hold

you against
your will

and I get giddy
feeling your captive

body as the harp-
sichord plays Bach.

FROM *REBEL LIONS*, 1984

Dark Brown Eyes of Seals

THE CRUNCH OF GUILT WITHIN THE NECK
BITES THE MUSCLES OF THE JAW
at memory's site of what is beautiful
of sexuality and bliss.
(This takes the silent, active shapes
of secrets deep within—and then we do not know
what is *out* or *here* or *in*.)
THE
MEMORY
itself
is an infant's phantasm—locked in living-out
a strangling or a luscious kiss
that swirls in dripping chocolate
and gentle hurricanes
of milky arms and breasts.
The unknown pseudopods entwine
to make our spirits into streaming jewels
just as each higher cell
has become a pulsing pirate chest
wherein we are sleeping wolves
and singing angel fools

and
all
this
coils

and intercoils

and we stand on tiptoe
to bend and see our heels.
The air we breathe with deepening breath
is alive with birth and death.

We're held by the living arms of gods,
and moving through the summer waves
we're watched
by dark brown eyes of seals.

Rose Rain

RAIN ON THE ROSES,
BLUE SKY,

and
you

on my
mind.

Nothing could be kinder.

I'm finding

the way.

Let's play
each day

like mayflies
in December

like stars

in the eternal
sky!

"To Glean the Livingness of Worlds"

replying to Rilke's Eighth Elegy

> Animals see the unobstructed
> world with their whole eyes ...
> But our eyes, turned back upon
> themselves, encircle and
> seek to snare the world,
> setting traps for freedom.
> The faces of the beasts
> show what truly IS to us.
> DUINO ELEGY
> NUMBER 8

I

NOW I'LL MAKE THIS MINE:

WITH EVERY EYE IN POUNDING SKULLS

BEASTS SEE THE OPENING.

That's not true.

Nor are they in some calm state
for a leap to someplace beyond the senses' field.
Theirs is a less mental shape
of cortex, brainstem and starry tissue
—and I have been there

I have dreamed there—in fleshy hell
hoping
to break time's tissue down
and thereby crumple space to bring a heaven
near to me.

(Me, I'll crumple space up
as all creatures do,
DIS-
SOLVING TIME.)

There's no clearing out there.
NO GLADE.

It is
all
ILLUMINED BY

the arms and teeth that made it

and the laugh and cry.

2

MY EYES WERE NOT TURNED BACK
UPON THEMSELVES
but went reaching out through all the wolves and elves
that slept beneath my bed and in the corners of my head

TO OUTWARD SWEEP
and draw my love brute back to me.

My eye were solid ghosts projected
where the world unfolds.

I see no separate oneness in the visages
of beasts
that is strange to me,
except that their clarity does not unfold
to whirl itself to fireworks
that blow my mind with lights

and with sights of this doe who stands beside
the street in bright headlights of my car
while her two plump, spotted fawns
blink toward my smile,

HEY YOU!

Hey deer, I'm on fire! You are more
comfortable,
at some moments, because your spirit
has fewer swirls and your conscious body

lives deeper back in time.

3

DEATH IS BESIDE THE POINT!
WE'RE ALWAYS DEAD

and

in

EVERY WAY
this flesh is every way alive. Our extinction

IS THE PROOF THAT WE ARE FLAMES

and the grass fire continues on, alighting
up the forest.
                    Deer, you and I are the same stuff
        —just slightly different mists of spirit.

I could almost be your lover.

You are almost mine.

We're Brother / Sister.

WHAT GLORY IS THIS UNIVERSE THAT THINKS!

I always become an animal
as you are always
BEING ONE;

it is one unfolding.

it is unfolding
one
to the other,
Sister, Brother.

4

BLACKBERRY BLOSSOMS ON THE VINE
and their fruits of pebbled black
and glinting red
reach out madly in the air

when not trimmed back

to accommodate
the garden of philosophy.

Layer after layer of thorny stalk and leafy stack
HURL THEMSELVES OUT
in sunny morning air
that vibrates with the cries
of mating hawks.

This is almost perfect imitation of the tiers
of stars creating us
from which we draw our juice
or blood

and on the fruit of which we clean our hooves
or tap our *fin de siècle* gloves.

SO MUCH FOR SAD PURE EMPTINESS!

SO MUCH FOR SAD PURE EMPTINESS!
where roses
bloom by castle walls.

5

THIS LIFE IS STAR LIFE;
                            SISTER DEER AND I
SEE STARS WITH STARS.
                            Brother puma
            bites his lover's neck and she sees
            multidimensioned
                            shapes of light.

        What is in space for roses and for berries
                        is the life
                    that's whirling there
                    WITHIN
            —within the organelles of cells

        and the imagined time they took to crumple selves

        into a racing thing that's standing in the rains
                and still beyond the reach of brains.

                NO ONE EVER

                    turned

                    my

                    HEAD

                    back

                to face away

        from the world in which I
                            die and play.

MY BODY IS PUT IN BOXES
and then the boxes are surrounded
by moving images of boxes
with myself inside of them, looking at the moving
picture, book and TV boxes.
These show those who approve
or disapprove
from their essential
teetering groundlessness in almost
unconnected boxes, and so forth,
on and on . . . till I might be deaf or dumb.

I MIGHT FORGET THAT I AM
a swirl of spirit
in an ebullient world!

AND THAT THERE IS JOY.

This is joy that I eat the sun-heated berry,
smell the rose, smile at the deer,
and flick my headlights off and on
to see if she will run.

There is pain if my fingers are pricked by thorns
or if I am crushed by cars or bombs
of if my flame is made to smolder
by a sopping blanket of what is numb.

IF I HAD A TRILLION SENSES
I COULD TELL YOU
why molecules are lies,

AND

WHAT

WE

TRULY

ARE

! ! !

—AND WHY WE BUILD THESE SOULS
and what is the perfume that they are!

.

If I had a thousand-trillion senses I could tell you
why molecules are lies
and
what
we
truly
ARE
! ! !

—And why we build these souls
and how
(if we may make one)
it may help to heal
the scar.

THE GARTER SNAKE IS THE SLEEKEST ANGEL
that I know, with his simple mind
that is inseparable from hunger
and an endless history,
whether in his spine or great black
gleaming eyes.
(He, like the sea beast beat by waves,
is the deep philosopher,
and not someone with shears
who carves out sculptured emptiness
among the scentless roses,
while pretending he can't smell.)

We're always there with death.
I'm made of death,
called *particles of matter,*
and that's one joy of life:
that I have beat out entropy
and am the whirlwind of a trembling strife.

I

HOLD

MY LOVER

in these arms
and she says my head is a sun
for her.
(Her breasts are universes lying on *my* arms.)

WE ARE EACH OTHER'S INSTRUMENT
to glean the livingness of worlds.
In each of us is something wild.
There are enough mild
dull eyes of domestic brutes that we have bred
from bird and beast
to make them part alive and partly dead.

A thousand generations in a cage
makes a helpless thing
—not even quaint
like bat-shaped cracks
in grandma's porcelain
or
moon shadows
thrown by basil on a garden wall.
The ecstatic hunger of the snake
is what I filter through this fox of reason
as I touch damp moss or steering wheel,
OR
LAUGH
AT
THE
SKY
which is a monster, living, baby cell

as am I,

or laugh at the sky
which is a monster, living, baby cell

as are you and I.

———————————

What we stare out upon or sniff
is the whale tooth in the ivory jaw
and the sandgrain in the pearl
reflecting back the myriadness
of this intermingling swirl.

Dark Contemplation

for Jay Defeo

"AGNOSIA"—DARK CONTEMPLATION,
let me kneel to thee, let me kneel to thee,
for I have become as shallow as a small stream
that trickles through the rocks and the clay
where the bunch grass grows and the sun-cups
open their petals and smile with their sex at the sky.
I know less than the small fly
who lands on the red-veined stone.
Now I am ready to know, for nothing is known.
My mind is a worn sheet of virulent vanities.
Each small step forward laughs
with the cynicism of tragedy
and I sense there is something
dark of me,
and I sense there is something
dark of me,
that must now be quiet
and silently roar

AND

I

WOULD

BOW MY HEAD

TO ALL THINGS

that I have never seen before

and to this creature in the cave

who blinks and sniffs in the sun.

I hear from long ago
that I and my thoughts are one.

Freewheelin's Tattoo

FRANK, HOW PLEASED
I AM
to see that Death's Head
tattoo of red and blue
blocked in
with solid black;
how good
to view the sign
of madcap finality
filled up
with darkness
to make a wing shape
forever flying
on your arm.
It
is
your new charm
or token
and it shows
that spirit cannot
be broken
but ever grows
toward flight.

FROM *SIMPLE EYES &*
OTHER POEMS, 1993

Spirit's Desperado

SPIRIT'S DESPERADO I, I CHEER AND BRAVO
THE SIDE OF NEGATION AND OF HUNGER
FOR SOUL.
As a boy I saw the mole
AND THE EAGLE
soaring and burrowing together
and imagined that love
was created of hair and of feather
that rubbed on the edge
of
the
vast ledge
of Sight, Sound, Taste, Touch—and of the Smell
of satin and silk, and of the guts
of the butchered creature
that writhes and grows a brain.
I was sure that it was not Hell
that I was living
but I was reflecting the stain
of that Huge Being
called
THE
STARS!!

I KNEW IT WAS NOT EVEN HEAVEN

BUT IT IS ALL-DIVINE!

To be alive is to feast on desperation!

Mexico Seen from the Moving Car

THERE ARE HILLS LIKE SHARKFINS
            and clods of mud.
The mind drifts through
in the shape of a museum,
in the guise of a museum,
dreaming dead friends:
Jim, Tom, Emmet, Bill.
—Like billboards their huge faces droop
and stretch on the walls,
on the walls of the cliffs out there,
where trees with white trunks
            make plumes on rock ridges.

My mind is fingers holding a pen.

Trees with white trunks
            make plumes on rock ridges.
Rivers of sand are memories.
Memories make movies
            on the dust of the desert.
Hawks with pale bellies
            perch on the cactus,
their bodies are portholes
            to other dimensions.

This might go on forever.

I am a snake and a tiptoe feather
at opposite ends of the scales
as they balance themselves
against each other.
This might go on forever.

The Butterfly

YELLOW AND BLACK,
    black and yellow . . . in a smooth flicker
the butterfly raises and lowers
her wings,
        in a smooth flicker,
    as she steps
    in an awkward walk
    like a dancer.
    She sips the taste of the mountain
    from the red-black mud,
    from the red-black mud
    near the river.

    The gray-silver clouds are ocelot spots
and a stone peak stares from a notch in green cliffs.

    She sips the taste of the mountain
    from the red-black mud
    and
    a cowbell rings
        in the shadow of clouds.

the Sierra Madre

The Cheetah

See the face
of a beautiful
  and highly
  intelligent
    child
      in
      the
    profile
of the cheetah.
    SHE
    IS
    BEYOND
    ALL
    GOOD
      and
EVIL
and more like us
than we can ever
imagine.

The black stripes
at the tip of her tail
twitch
and she closes her eyes
as my mother used to do,
with pleasure.

Her three large kittens
nod and grin in the sun.

What is human
is so much more obvious
in beings with tails.

Samburu, Kenya

STANZAS FROM
DOLPHIN SKULL, 1995

THIS CLOUD IS A LIFE as the great horned owl hoots
three calls. The pony of memory tramples the rattlesnake.
Sunset colors of apricot and layers of black
over the ocean. A puff of summer dust where
the buckeye butterfly lands. Mystic wings
of planets and scarlet nebulae. A lock
on the machine gun under the bed.
FACES
TWISTED
in
pain
from the old times when love hurt
so much that it is spotlights
filled with legs and mouths
writhing.
Nylon stockings filled with sentimental songs
are stained with blackberry juice like
my fingers.
AND
I
LOVE
YOU,
your blue eyes.
Crinkle of frost on the windows. This
is all fog off the ocean coming over
the line of brown hills.
TAILGATING
DRIVERS
behind me
with stoic faces
of Arnold Schwarzenegger.
The city is a mammal vision
in peaks of fog.
Jack Pumpkinhead is laughing with the Tin Man
and
an

AXE
chops through it all
showing the dry grain
                    and the whorls.
Raphael found the rules and was freed.

.

THE CLOUD THAT RAPHAEL FOUND is the rules of freedom.
Dark green shamrocks grow in a bowl where
dead friends live in dreams. Sounds of blue-black
jays screaming. My arm around Robert helping
him into my car. "Crazy John's new book
is like your poetry," I say, showing him
                    the fine printing.
"How?" "It's the elegance," I answer.
The gray-brown moth flutters
O
V
E
R
the brick-red and scarlet and blue
of the prayer rug.
YOU,
your blue eyes
the daintiness of your ankle,
your deep wit,
these are the reasons I am alive.
Miró knows it is all play and Pollock understands
the unconscious power.

NOW

THERE

ARE

LIONS

IN

THE

WOODWORK.

Now I smell my Grandma as she looks
at me through her thick glasses.
Now I understand the sexual addiction
of my young manhood
was a CRUCIFIXION—
glittering and lovely
AS
an ostrich boa and smashed mirrors

seen on acid.

■

STICK FIGURES OF JACK AND JILL. Figures of Jack and Jill
and the teacher's face like a huge moth in midair.
Billy Goats Gruff look at the pattern
on the wings. Red and brown
planets with auras and the miraculous pitcher.
Crayfish in ponds under bridges.
A dead friend's eyes through
his wire-rim glasses.
His laugh has become part of my bones.
THIS
CITY
OF
MY HEART
was once innocent as a baby and we
grew up in it.   Shoe shops.   Bakeries.   Umbrella shops
in department stores.
Seasons of heavy rains and babies.   Cold silver
wings.   Steaming food on a wooden table.

EX
TREMES
OF
POVERTY.
Agonies over the rent.
FACES
TWISTED

BY

LOVE

IN

THE
NIGHT.
BODIES
tearing
at
one
another
like sleek figures
high
on the drugs of our glands.
And still we are all gods and I have a huge face.

■

I AM A GOD WITH A HUGE FACE.   Lions
and eagles pour out of my mouth.   Big white
square teeth and a red-purple tongue.   There are
magenta clouds around my head and this
is my throne room.   Actors perform
the drama of my being inside of you,
WEARING
YOUR
SKIN.
I

am

writing and clawing.
BEG FOR MERCY.
Blackberry bramble catching
my pants leg.   A tearing sound.
Deep inside in the padded car.
Garbage truck full of petroleum fantasies.
Dogs barking under the dark
tall pine trees.   Hollyhocks
and a few pink roses.   You are
everyone
BUT
I am nobody.
Nobody is very large
and
powerful.
Memory is naked bodies
in a battle.   The war is sensuous
as a little boy's penis.
Fighter planes are guns.
I am the river god
in love with my dreams.
Not dreams but ongoing presences
spewed from the bang
through a nervous system.
At the edge of things but reaching
way back inside.

■

HOLD, LET THIS MOMENT never cease. Drag it out
of context look at the roots of it in quarks
and primal hydrogen. It's the sound
of Shelley's laugh in my ears.
YOU
THINK
WE

ARE
BODIES
WALKING
UP   Kissing.
TO   Holding hands.
ONE
ANOTHER
AND
SPEAKING.
A universe before man ever was, filled
with dragonflies
in
your
eardrums.
Palm trees and skyscrapers. Vervet monkey
in the euphorbia tree staring at me.
The lion is consciousness. The eagle
is experience. As real as mud
chiming
with light
from
rainbows.
"Fuck you," right in your face.
"Fuck you!" He pulls out a gun
in reply. Gun the size of a toilet.
Blue-black. Bullets fire into a world
made of stacks of dirty feet.
Eyes of starving families. Dust
from red clay. Something
is purring
or flying.
Sound of thunder jars loose dead leaves
and they slowly fall
while the bell rings.

■

THE OLD RABBIT BEGINS TO WINK, then the pony
tramples the rattlesnake. Eagle bones in a dream.
The eternal dimensions before the bang
have closed themselves off. This one
tries to be the realm of entropy.
Sombreros the color of children's
cookies. Colorlessness at the edges
of things. Radiances of blue-silver
clouds and mountain ranges
of cool white fog. I'm in a black suit
with wide legs. You. You are elegant
with soft arms
and strong fingers.

THERE

IS

JOY

IN

THE

ROOM

sometimes and
it is the field of complex
presences.

Big clear laughs are the best
and deep seeing eyes
looking back through the muscles
of mastodon hunters
out
towards
the edge of the solar system
and a wall of surprising stars.
All of this through the background
BLUR

of one-dimensionality,
psyche projections,
and vibrancies of the substrate
as it turns
itself inside-out like a protein.

FROM *RAIN MIRROR*, 1999

From *Haiku Edge*

OH ACCIDENT !

Oh,

per

fect

((CRUSHED))

snail

— LIKE

A

STAR

gone out

!

■

HEY, IT'S ALL CON

SCIOUSNESS

— thumps

of assault

rifles

and

the

stars

■

PINK BANDAID STUCK
to the asphalt
looks gray
in
moon
light

while
crick
ets
sing

∎

MOLDY
BOARD
smell
!
((AH))
My
Grand
pa's
face
appears
in
the air

∎

BRASS
and
turquoise

—and
smell
of
pine boards
in
the
rain

∎

OH

HUM
MING
BIRD
SHAD
OW
on the black
plum
!

((No summer lightning
though))

∎

Hey
DRIVER,
your
big,
soft,
steel,
rubber-smelling
car

owns you

∎

for James Broughton

THE DRY
fir needle
rolling
in
the wind

has

a

shad

ow

∎

THE FOX TURD
is a cliff
a
n
d
the
butterfly
is
a
condor

■

THE HERON
flies quickly
o
ver
your head
as you speak
on the
phone

■

ORION
through
the bare
branches;
the leaves
are on
the
ROOF

∎

BEFORE DAWN
the train whistle
quivers
like
a
SAIL
made of stars

∎

for Bruce Conner

BUTTERFLIES
swirling madly.
Ah,
light shows
at the Avalon!

From *Crisis Blossom*

for Amy,
by my side,
each footstep,
every taste,
each touch

grafting one

NOW I UNDERSTAND THE SEXUAL ADDICTION
of my young manhood
was a CRUCIFIXION—
glittering and lovely
AS
an ostrich boa and smashed mirrors
seen on acid.

Now
I see that perception is a shape
of the darkness
S
E
E
I
N
G
itself.
Naked bodies in layers
on shelves in space,
and behind stalactites,
alight with themselves
seduce me
with fleshly softness
of their meat.
Calves.
Forearms.
And the perfumes!

THE PERFUMES ARE LOST
AS MOTHS
IN OUR HORMONAL STORMS
but they direct us.
—They guided me.

grafting two

MY
GOD   MY GOD!

NO   MY GOD!

don't   MY GOD!

DO
THIS

to me!

DON'T DO THIS TO ME!

I've looked down into it
and I come back
with my eyes
glazed.
My eyes glazed.
That twig has a rabbit's head!
The orange flesh of the apricot
where the mouth bites it
is a Hell/Heaven
a Hell/Heaven
of naked figures.
The brown dimples of the Bay,
as the plane lands,
are a horse's back.
DON'T DO THIS TO ME!
I love it!

I AM A GOD WITH A HUGE FACE. Lions
and eagles pour out of my mouth. Big white
square teeth and a red-purple tongue. There are
magenta clouds around my head and this
is my throne room. Actors perform
the drama of my being inside of you,
WEARING
YOUR
SKIN.
Our
hunger

is

greater

than
our fear.
My shoe slips
on the red brick that is coated
with slime of algae and moss
and the same fear that is ever there makes a hollyhock
in the darkness
where water moths with billowing antennae
and black velvet heads vie
in midair for the senses of their ladies.
A
SMALL
POEM
is a soul
like an opal.

grafting nine

YOU ARE MY MEMORIES OF YOU

holding my hand.

I

WANT

TO

GO

ANYWHERE.

I am a flowering.

YOU MAKE ME A THOUGHT-DIVER,

elastic

and

miraculous

in every deed

and sniff and laugh

I've ever done.

EACH SOFT TOUCH

and toothed cruelty

is embedded

in the dream structure

OF

THIS

STUFF

that

turns

into something

too much like stone.

above Santa Fe, New Mexico

grafting fourteen

WATER BOILS IN THE BIG COPPER TUB. White sheets
will be dipped in the blueing. Wrung out in the wringer
and then hung up to dry. THE SUBSTRATE IS SO VIBRANT
that I can't get close to it. It is YOU. YOU who are
as the owl hoots.

FIRST
we experiment with selves, the imprints
that we invent before us—of feathering touch,
of lips to breasts, of piano making notes being Haydn,
silk quilts, slash of wind in the snowstorm, taste of black cherry,
yellow olive oil floating in sour cream
with the flesh of herring.
—From that falls out
the possibility
of the numinous.
HOPE.
Unease.
Small, shining, sizeless
triumphs
like knots
in oak roots
rest on the ground
with dandelions and grasses around.
Even *skandhas*
have
skandhas.
Agnosia
goes blind.
Hummingbirds with pink-gold breasts
and a red full moon is rising.

bud

HEARTACHE NEWS WITH THE TORTURED FACES
and grim boredom verging on insolence,
and a rifle slung over the shoulders.
Lines of meaningless glyphs slither past
beneath a band of silver
ON
BLACK.
THE SALMON MUST KNOW
how to find its stream,
and the absence of thorns
I
S
the absence
of odor. Perfume
the color of pink-tinted pewter.

C
H
I
L
D
R
E
N
smile in the bodies
of grownups.
A
H
!

Cleveland

grafting eighteen

FACES
TWISTED
in pain
from the old times when love hurt
so much that it is spotlights
filled with legs and mouths
writhing.
It is all like the painted scroll
of garish ghosts having a wedding.
One of them with a misshapen face
is selling a chubby fox, bound
with silver cords
and lying on a stool,
to another ghost
who leans forward,
fascinated.

E
X
A
C
T
L
Y,

and there are hummingbirds
and physical pains flying around one another
and looping
in big free patterns.

above Nebraska
—remembering a scroll in
the Cleveland Museum of Art

MIRÓ KNOWS IT IS ALL PLAY AND POLLOCK UNDER-
STANDS
the unconscious power.
CONSCIOUSNESS
RISES
UP
in a green wave
with a darting grebe,
neck outstretched and wings like fins,
fishing in the crest.
The beach sun behind
makes it a sculpture.
THE WIND
AND GRAVEL
stir shapes
of uprising reason.
EARS,
EYES, NOSE, TONGUE,
grow rich to accept such carving

AND

WE

ARE

BLANK SPOTS

OF

BLACKNESS
sprouting tiny, many-colored flowers.

during Haydn quartet

flower

"GIVE WAY OR BE SMITTEN INTO NOTHINGNESS
and everlasting night." But I am here already,
the tips of my fingers give off light.
What matters is the cold skin of the python
and her muscled ribs
that ripple over the crate. One band
of power preceding another. There is
ZERO,
and the nonstructure of nada inside.

EVERY

THING

is

FULL

BLAST

in its glory.

A
CLOUD
of protein
made of
protein's imagination
in the spark of a star.

Bali

From *After the Solstice*

"GIVE WAY OR BE SMITTEN INTO NOTHINGNESS
and everlasting night."
But I am here already,
the tips of my fingers
give off light.

FROM THIS WINDOW:
a sea lion glides in the trough
of the river by the ocean
and
MY
CHILDHOOD
LOOMS
WITH

MY
DEATH

AT

THE
CORE

AND
MY
FUTURE

LIES

with my

DEATH

IN
STORE
and
sea palms
bend and snap
with crash of surf
on the rock

.   .   .   .   .

THERE'S
ME

and no me

on the other side

I'm here under my hand

AND
THERE

where thoughts glide.

STARS

OF

NEURONS

DRIZZLE

FROM *PLUM STONES:*
CARTOONS OF NO HEAVEN, 2002

Plum Stone Two

FOG. FOG AROUND RAINBOWS
RAINBOW IN CLEAR LIGHT
HORSE HEADS LIKE EAGLES.
EAGLES LIKE HORSE HEADS

Z

O

O

M

I

N

G

through
STORMS.
BIG DROPS SPLASHING
ON THE REDWOOD DECK RAIL

INNER AND OUTER REALM MATED
IN SIZELESSNESS
Rainbows pouring in water falls
WATER FALLS GURGLING IN STREAMS
OF CHILDHOOD.

COMPASSION SWIRLING THROUGH MERCY

BIRTH

GOES

OUT

WITH

A

LIGHT BULB

Always here
in continuous practice:
a brown moth resting on old lace,

and a can of peaches
in tommorrow's firelight

PLUM.
Somewhere a plum is ripe.
Swirling like horse heads
in rainbows.

Purple plum.

Green plum.
Blue-black edging through white
with hands in prayer.

O
R
D
I
N
A
R
Y

as palm
pressed to palm
in
a
mudra.

BOWING
IN BLESSING
after all
these
years.

A PLUM IS RIPE.

COLD HARD GOLD-BROWN PEARS
in the rain
by the eaves

alert with bare
branches

like kitten fur and deer eyes
plain as a skid mark.
ORDINARY,
ORDINARY AS BOWING
IN BLESSING.
Z
O
O
M
I
N
G
through
STORMS.
EAGLES LIKE HORSE HEADS.
HORSE HEADS LIKE EAGLES.
FOG. FOG AROUND RAINBOWS
like kitten fur and deer eyes
plain as skid marks.
ORDINARY

ORDINARY AS BOWING
IN BLESSING.
O
R
D
I
N
A
R
Y

as palm
pressed to palm
in
a
mudra

Plum Stone Six

VAIN. VANITY. VANITAS.
AS A BLACK RIVER IS VAIN
WITH WHITE ROCKS.
V
A
N
I
T
Y
makes
THUNDER
in soft flesh
imagining nothingness

THE GLEAMING FACE,
HELD HIGH, DESCENDS
TO THE CROWD.
DRAGON SLAYER ARRIVES;
blue-silver waves crash loud.
Water lashes and swirls.

The same story rolls over
and over
giving meat
to
another
body.

.

C
O
M
P
A
S
S
I
O
N,
O WISE ONE,
for these scattering skulls
and crude jagged stones.
Bring quiet to Lorca
and the unending memories
of tiny black beetles,
and pink seaweed
of crusty coral
at
the
shallow edge
of the pool;

ALL,
ONE.

A black river is vain
with white rocks.
VANITY. VANITAS.
WISDOM. COMPASSION.
In the smile of the dragon,
in the slayer
and the slain.
Mouse tracks on the snow
pictured in childhood books
and screams
in the air.

PALM

JOINED

TO

PALM

HEAD

BENT

IN

A

BOW

I

LOVE

YOU,

O

N

E

L

A

Y

E

R

of belief

hiding another

I

SWIRL

AT THIS CENTER

with folded legs

while the rooster crows

VANITY. VANITAS.

A black river is vain
with
white
rocks

ALL,
ONE

Plum Stone Fifteen

WELCOME DEAR CHAOS.
WELCOME LIGHT
OF THE ROAR.
CALM LIGHT OF THE ROAR.
SOUND OF A FEATHER
FALLING
IN SOME PARADISE.
PARADISE NEARBY.

R
O
A
R

L
I
G
H
T
in
ordinary
BLACKNESS.

TRANSPARENT
B
L
A
C
K
N
E
S
S
ZINGS
out and in.

Sculptured hands
of a seated figure.
Half-closed eyes.
Plain as disturbance and straw
and Grandpa's tin snuff box.

NO LIGHT

NO STRAW

NO DONKEY

Even dada failed.

The sutra rests on a lotus.
One hand swings the sword.
Flame edges are blades,
chopping out walls
freeing the realms.
Serious as comedy.
CARTOONS OF NO HEAVEN.
Where is a beginning or end?
Tied up in string and star cliffs?
No beginning or end.

Cartoons of no heaven.
Straw and Grandpa's snuff box.
The mind in the hands knows.
HERE.
Six trillionths of a moment.

Sometimes a Stan Brakhage film
projected on the skin
of a tadpole;
more
often
WISDOM
DISGUISED
AS
COMPASSION.

Roaring in the four corners.
The center is unutterably calm,
and does not seem so
before birth flashes
lightning and turquoise.
We sit on black cushions
in
the
C
O
O
L
N
E
S
S

■

WE SIT ON BLACK CUSHIONS
IN
THE
C
O
O
L
N
E
S
S;

I SIT IN NO BODY
BUT ALL THINGS

THEY INTERMIX
MAKING NO SPLENDOR
or hangings of red velvet

∎

PLUM.
Somewhere a plum is ripe.
Swirling like horse heads
in rainbows
IT
IS
ALL ORDINARY
as star light
sparkling
on
ivory
and

paint catching fire

in a car crash

as

I cross

the stream

Unchanged

NO MEAT, NO MIND, NO CONSCIOUSNESS,

NO ONE TO BE FREE OF DARKNESS

OR FOR THE LIGHT TO FIND IN UNIVERSES OF WHITE EAGLE

WINGS—WHERE I HAVE BEEN WITH YOU!

With no regret we will leave

as if we

WERE NEVER HERE

holding it precious and perfect

IN THE ONGOING NOTHINGNESS

(((^^^^

^^^^^^^^^^))

BORN AND UNBORN, TASTES OF DARK CHOCOLATE,

touch of lavender cashmere,

NOT EVEN KNOWING

there's nothing

to

forget

—even tired arm muscles after swimming.

THIS IS OUR PERFECTION

SWIRLS IN ASPHALT

for Amy

The limits of the knowable are unknowable.
DŌGEN ZENJI, THIRTEENTH CENTURY

A FOREST OF HORSES
is where I am
IN
YOUR
EYES
and you have
handed
me your love
with your
smiles and tears
and my heart
in my mouth
knows we are
still babes
and innocents
dancing on
the edge
of impermanence
as it moves
rapidly
and
torturously
but
we
will always
survive
just like
this
in
(this)
moment.
THE LOOK ON YOUR
FACE
assures me.

NO MORE FEROCITY
for lunch;
the shadows
of teeth
are enough
to frighten
tiny
creatures
into trembling
and the shakes.
The tall purple
irises at the door
to the cave
are
a torch
lit to honor
us if
we sleep there
on the heaps
of gold coins.
But I would rather
kiss
your
finger
in our hideout
than be rich
for ten trillion years
where the lion roars.

3

I POLISHED THE STARS
off my boots.
They're skin now.
Faces of Rembrandt
and Shakespeare
on their tops
speak
to
one another.
Covered with
the comedy
of bruises
and torn nails.
Smell of lime
from the squeezed
RIND
mixes with stardust
settling around
the rusty
refrigerator
lying
on the hill.
We are
here
in the car roar
in
this instant
between the changing
of climates
and the love
we claim
with our
infinite
presences.

THE MOMENT IS OUR
real body
as are all moments
mutually arising
together.
Your eyes
are moonrise.
Each moment
is the gate
of emancipation.
Swelling with pride
I'm
here
with dark hair
in a green Scottish
jacket
to see the eagle
flying over
with the dead
gazelle calf
in her claws
while the jackal
runs beneath her
jumping
and
barking.
THERE
ARE
NO
LESSONS
but the waves
in your hair.

5

HOW BADLY
we need love
to
invent
it.
WE
pretend to
be
billowing clouds
of flesh
giving morning
kisses
on the backs
of our necks.
WE
ARE
(floating)
SUSPENDED
I
N
honey
like
cupids
in amber.
Listen,
the whales
are singing
very clearly
in our hearts
and there's a blade
of violet light
on the window
ledge.

6

WE GO THROUGH THIS
not to be
here. Reflected
in star light
is
the
only
truth.
It's plain
as a brown checkered
lizard hiding
behind a rock.
We
love this being
HERE.
Pretending is as real
as our bodies
BEING
GATES OF LIBERATION
and
not knowing
which way
is pride
and which is sorrow.
Don't be sentimental
about samsara
especially autumn
and those vibrant
BLUE MORNING
GLORIES
growing
over the rose vine.

read at Peter Coyote's ordination

The moment does not
require
knowing
if breath is going
in or out.
The bell hammer
is wrapped in
faded velvet
from the curtain
of a play.
Two dumb
proud
actors
never
go
away.
Just shouting
and cooing
and cursing,
always
divine
and
not.
And we are skinny
black silhouettes
walking on cold
sand
like the distant
Robert Creeleys
at the surf
edge.

I LOVE SPEAKING
through the monkey's
mouth.
But
not
to
you.
You are real.
We remember
mountains and solstice nights
where the water
runs forever
through the icy
pipe
and at last
bursts out
flashing light
and steaming
IN
THE
INSTANT.
Here
we rub
ourselves
against
countless
gates
of liberation.
The mountains
are out there
being interviewed.
Forget this is a vigil.

9

IF WE GO ONE STEP
further
we will really
be
here
beyond
meat
and
imagination.
Your buttocks
are finer than
french metaphors.
Truly we will
be HUNGRY
and quietly
intoxicated
and in love
with mint flowers
and powerful glossy
big shouldered
trucks —
AND
HEAR
GREAT
VOICES
in the air
like Mayan
kings and queens
whose
dwarfs stare
into obsidian mirrors.
Right

here
on these
soft old
sheets
in their beatness.

THE CAT LIES AGAINST
my bare arm while
the train whistles
in the fog.
Firelight in darkness.
A dot of hugeness
chambered
by movies.
All about
are the Tanzanian
plains
with an ostrich
egg sitting
up in the
pale
pink-yellow
sundown.
Anything
to cover over
the agony
— especially
butternut squash
soup
and sardines
on a plate.
The pain is
CHILD'S
MAGIC
drunk on
the vistas
of weathered
skin

and wrinkles
and
the cat's fur
stiffens
as the fire crackles.

THE "CONTINGENT FLUX"
is a nugget
of turquoise
set in gold
or the black
spider
darting out
from under
the cutting board
and back
again.
The TOTAL of life
like the waterfall
does
not
feel pain.
Though safe,
each of us suffers.
The moment
is soft,
luxurious
fur
making a cavern
or a
a
pristine
shelter
of the senses
and non senses,
filled
with revelation
as
soft
and perfect
as your hand.

"BLIND SEEING"
surrounds
the divine,
BREAKS THE KNOT
and floats like neon
in the mist.
It's painted on a letter
in an arcane
book.
Eyes decorate
this page
staring
at the smoke
of consciousness,
BUT
NO
CLUES.
The
moment
is
clogged
with bandaged
thoughts
and testosterone.
The frisson
that comes
with cold
nakedness
is here in
the wet
cold clay.
The train whistle
is also
alive,
with
us.

IN THE PAINTED CHAMBER
with the niches
is a moment
of the passion
we embody,
AND
OUR
TIREDNESS
and
rest
and calm.
A cardboard bucket
of popcorn
and car crashes
is with us in
the darkness
and the waterfall.
The loud noise
is all around
in universal directions
and we are warmly touching.
You float
down the long
carpeted flight
— a movie goddess
in high sandals.
WE
belong.
This space
is our
nation.
Elsewhere
are stars
and sunlight.

IMAGINATION ENABLES
inspiration
to breathe into
the fingers
and
spine.
It
slashes barriers
with a forgiving
sword.
The songs
of the crickets
stop
as
eggs
are laid into
the coolness
underground.
In the night
we have
hours of the wolf
and yell
in
rage.
Torturing bodies
is becoming
the way
of the world
and it
intrudes
chilling our hearts.
A friend
narrates over
the soundtrack
of a TV movie

while a single tiny
jellyfish
polyp becomes a medusa
— and beats —
pulls away
from the pillar
of
its multiple selves
and swims
on the powerful
wing
of its body.

CASCADING SYNAPSES
don't explain
the black sparks
in the baby bird's
eyes,
and this instant
you look like
CALVIN
of
CALVIN AND HOBBES.
I
AM
SO
MOVED
to my depths
of flesh and nervous
system
and useless soul.
WE
ARE
STRANGE
LOVING
BRUTAL
CREATURES.
No,
not "brutal"
but with hungers
for meat and fish
and triumphs.
All spaces are filled
by
personalities
and big blobs
of new love.

I STRIKE OUTWARDS
to choke
my dead stepfather
in the dream —
only
sixty years
have passed
and
he
is
new
in a white
snap button
cowboy shirt.
Denouncing me
he steps from
the waterfall.
Mosquitoes brush,
bumping
my ear
below the volcano.
Naked, smiling
at me
you have
ripples.
YOU CALL
HORSES
and they gallop to you.
We are always
here
where
I
am inside out.
Thrilled

with animals
coming into
BEING
by
torch light
on
glazed
walls.

17

MUSK   CRAB   SHELL
roses, warm
autumn breeze
are
part
of the BIG FIRE.
We burn
pass and change.
Adagio is too fast
for this "paramecium pace,"
zinging into senses
forgotten
and reborn.
Perfumes decorate
warm flesh.
Words and sensoria
are the body
of the moment.
Remembering New York
and the artists hotel
where a Russian
poet is
mugged in
the hall.
JUST
YOU
AND
I
here
waiting
for Hermes
with
his

message
and rainbows.
He steps through
the wall.
No one denies us.

18

O LION HEAD, UPLIFT ME
in this shapeless space.
Let me be brave as Philip
of Macedon
and Philip Whalen, Son of the Wolf.
The darkness
in the moment
is an elevator
to the peak
of the mountain
seen from our deck
through the oaks.
The silence (to the ear)
is a rainbow
to
the
pads
of the fingers
as the petals
of the red and white
streaked lily
are a carpet
to numb
soles.
THE BODY
OF STUFF
is clots
of evasive
superstrings
AND
THIS
LOST
DIMENSION
is

our hideout.
Hands like
yours
MUST
BE
IMMORTAL!

19

FROM THE PEAK
we see back here,
looking out
from where we are
always.
A HUGE DEAD
TRUCK
under swaying
tall trees. Just the same
for a thousandth
of a spark.
A
plain miracle
and bathed
in peace.
JUST OVER
THE HORIZON
the *mappa* world
boils
in a cauldron
with burgers
and phosphorus
and suet and steaming
propaganda juice,
with families dying of thirst.
TOUCH
THIS
LUXE
SILK
RUG
with tribal patterns
of Central Asia.
How

perfect
to be
with you
where there are
birds.

20

THE FOREST OF HORSES
is a floating
island
in the eye
and
the inner retina
is always
A MOON'S
reflections.
Under the toes
is a mattress
OR
A FOREST.
The doctor's office
is looming
yellow
and smells like shots
and grimed paintings
in Roman
churches.
There is my
death cry
as the bullet
enters
on the radio,
BLINKING OUT
my sensoria;
eyes and ears
have
a second birth
before they paddle
the blue river
and splash

THE WATERFALL.
Light sources
are dayglo saffron
and brightly
RED-VIOLET.

21

SAMHAIN.
Fallen leaves,
smoke and a little
dampness
AND
THE
MOMENT
OF RAIN.
Big drops
OUTDOORS
jiggle
on the phone wire.
Egyptian beads
cast into shapes
of winged pharaohs.
I
WANT
the statue
of a boulder
with runes
carved in the Hebrew alphabet.
Your impassive glance
leaves me more
trembling than frost.
Smell the combusted
diesel
in fog.
We
are
in
a
ROMANTIC
LANDSCAPE
by the steep side

of Dōgen Creek
not far from the graffiti'ed
warehouses
and voices
of the mystical forest.

SWIRL OF ASPHALT
in warm wet
fog.
A
GOLDEN DAWN
in an unknowing
cloud
creates deep tunnels
and caves where babies
sing in the moment.
IT IS EXACTLY
MYTHOLOGY
when children
are our dark
muscles.
I have joined
you
and instincts
and hormones
are
interactions of
glucose and gases
AND
IF
there is
another place
or instant
I will not
receive it
FOR
LIPS
kissing you
make true gold
and true ivory
and there is amber
around your neck.

RIGHT HERE
WE ARE NOT IMAGES
but fountains.
From the half-blind
instant
we build
molecular jewels:
twisting,
opening, and zipping
shut,
IN
UNIVERSAL
DIMENSIONS,
and wound among bodies
of stars
where a mattress
of new green
MOSS
on a craggy
stone
(under the deck)
is twinned
with the scent
of a half
open rose.
YOU
KNOW
ME
by my
fingers
on your soft
arm

while
you
give
KISSES
to the cat.

PLATFORMS OF WHITENESS
and cairns made
of visions
are thrown
in the backpack
of thought.
Ordinary
as a salamander
or a maroon chevy.
We build
a useless soul
and are sane
in the moment
of
endlessly overlapping
WARS
feeling the crazed
shaking
and hearing
the bloody sweat
bubble
as arms and bodies
change into snakes.
The SCREAMING
in the presentfuture
is
GOOD
as cheesecake
and
MOLTEN LAVA.
We hold it
together
with just our bodies.
Let our nerves
be tutored.

MUSCLE   TISSUE   TENDON
teased
into mind-waves
IS
AN
INSTANT
of incense
and candle flame
suspended in beeping
yellow truck sounds.
I would like to sleep
in the shadowed grace
of the profile
of your nose
AND BROWS.
To the deepest
pit
a hummingbird
is a giant.
I
HAVE
abandoned it
all
for a misunderstanding
of
Chivalry,
BUT
RIGHT
HERE
IS THE GLEAM
OF
THE GRAIL.

ZINGING INTO SENSES
forgotten
and reborn
through
the body bardos.
BEING
thrums lightly
as rain
AND RISES
UPWARD THEN DOWNWARD
making cold pools
in streetlights
and subway gleams
and reflected headlights.
Beautiful faces
on the screen reward
US
with lives
less
complex
than this moment
AND MAKE
COLOR-CAVERN SPACES
that we fill
with our pleasure.
Believe
me,
your
perfect nipples,
your waist
and belly and blue
eyes
are born
each morning
where there are
morning glories.

I SAVE MYSELF
WITH THE NATURE
of my own body.
The treasure layer
of this moment
is a trillion feet
DEEP.
Excavating through
blind and ignored pleasures
we laugh without smiling
or grinning.
HOW
CAN
WE
bear this
is the question
nobody asks.
Every direction
is the step
to freedom,
through the waterfall.
Such ease
is impossible
AND
GROWS
on the big bones
of being rich.
Beyond our dreams
we see over the edge
into ourselves.
How ornate
is simplicity!

Lamantia

LAMB   SALMON   PRAWN
alive in me as
the dark chunky chocolate.
IT
NEEDS
TO BE
MESSY
like devouring life
"devouring" life.
All digestible materials
make neurons
and dendrites
to invent a messiah
with real feet
of fire hydrants and
palm trees and Fujiyamas
where we have breathed
cool air and listened
to monkeys
in the forest
IN
THIS MOMENT
and not now or future
or
never.
Here's the texture
of a tiny dry
brown leaf
brushed
from an old
wool
sweater
and

this
small
GOLD
NUGGET
on the floor.

PROUD OF TESTOSTERONE
and the chivalrous
ear-tingling, head-buzzing
SLOW OR SWIFT
sweaty sparkle
of the thrills in darkness
of meat and reason
and sunshine and shadow.
It is inside-out
in the moment
and it makes much
mammalian
REASON
when our bodies
touch in sizeless
pleasure.
There's the smell
of cedar
intermingling
with lavender
into a nonsense scent
holding the masked thoughts
of hummingbirds
at the feeder
and flat black blobs
that dart in the eye.

THE KERNEL OF EACH
BEING
is in the moment
with genomes
of frenzies and loves
MAKING
A
LIVING
MODEL
cued to become
less than it was
when it clustered
SO
SMOOTHLY
into protein presences:
ARMS AND LEGS,
RIPPLES
OF
abdomen.
HUNGER BODIES
swirl
into morphs
engulfing
the bulks
they create.
A
R
T
A
U
D
knew
this
when it rose up

through his floor.
We sleep
with it
happily
with our toes touching
in dreams.
Warm Caribbean waves
spread from the November
bouquet.

I

AM

(MERELY)

SANE
on this day
of the solstice night
in nazi America.

BREADTH OF BEING
in reason and action
are not less strange
than the tusked face
of a frenzied troll.
These are two of the seventeen
sides of striving
for godhead;
let me
not
destroy
this occasion,
spot,
occurrence,
with
BEING WHAT
HAS BEEN PLACED
upon me
by propaganda and big lies
and my own naked
discoveries
and radiant delusions
in furs and swift chariots
and plastic running shoes.
It is all just a single moment
to the pot of azaleas
with roots creating the caves
THEY MAKE
among countless blissful, earthy lives
of nematodes
and tiny smiling visages.
Our friends near the ocean
watch bobcats
being flames of spirit.

THE SUNSET MOMENT
IS AN ORANGE NEBULA
UPON
BLACK BLUENESS
shaking trees and the most distant
BLAZARS
in their sizelessness.
Consciousness and size
are oatmeal and rubber bands
compared to what we hug
between us
loving ourselves with
the momentary stuff.
It causes me much grief
that only the mere
bright instant
in the endless numbness
shall always be eternal
as your black parka
or our hands holding hands.
Soon there will be
yellow pansies
in the field of green grass
among the new deaths of old friends.
BUT
NOW
THE DAYS
GROW
LONGER
and bee queens
awaken
in their dark
winter
nests,
ready to imagine children
and nectar.

CHILDREN ARE CASUALTIES
of the sequential alignment
of moments into what
they are not meant to be
by the Nothingness
kissing their wings in flight.
IN A CRASHING
OF IMAGINATION, we witness
the hollowness
left here in the shapes
of things.
Goodbye like *Hello*
is more potent
THAN
ever wished for.
The Tin Man
continues creaking
and the Lion shaking
and stuttering
as they stand
on snow or sun-beaten sand
and not on
the muscles of instants
strung together.
IT
IS
TOO EASY TO TAKE!
Far too easy to take.
Too easy to take,
like the clear
thin, silver ring

of a tiny bell.
Without even being here
you and I chant farewell
to these bodies that shall
not grow more.

Jamie

for Sterling Bunnell

WE SWIM IN THE ILLUMINATION
of the full moon
through the cold
eucalyptus branches
AND
THE
CAT
really does purr somewhere
besides in our heads,
as real as the icy wind over
the garbage bin
and the smell of baked apples
and hot cinnamon.
We love the cold air that enters us
and the warm beaches
all wrapped in this moment.
Monteverdi voices sing:
"Hawk's breath on the table
and plums nestled in velvet."
It is carved on a jewel
with gyrfalcons diving
from their nest on a splintering cliff
to kill a lurking raven
with one blow of the beak
to her black cranium.
And I pick up the dead body
from the frozen moraine
and listen uncomprehendingly
to my friend's voice
shouting in the wind.
We are always together
IN THIS NEVER
which is the now

that we have
in whatever realms
we slip into from sleepiness
to dreams
that we remember
of those who come to speak to us
or mumble
right before waking.

35

A VULTURE FLIES OVER THE EDGE
of the pine
into an ancient sonata
of blue sky.
The city ceaselessly roars
in the mid-distance
and we might be lions
looking for the meaning
of things in themselves.
Secretly knowing this moment
is tentative
we put our feet
down on it
and it is as solid
as everything
ELSE.
We are dressed
in casual elegance
and our minds
melting
together are elegant.
The instant rushes
so rapidly in the citron silver car
that there is almost
NO LOVE
as it gives way to mutual
care and support,
NOT
ENOUGH
to go on living for.
THIS
HUNGER
is for itself
and only my chest

longing for you can suppress it.
You are beyond all,
in your laughter
and quietness,
and the way you imitate
the expressions of animals.

36

LIQUID MERCURY IN THE PALM
of my hand
is a presence
moving swiftly
to muse with the yellow sulfur
and young daydreams.
Nothing is as awesome
as the naked brown skin
of your back
and the apparitions
we have of success
and winning ourselves away
from this act finally.
We are not angels or neon
but we are visions at the prow
OF THE WAVE.
Look, no reason to fear
THE WEAKLY MURDEROUS
and
the murderous weaklings.
We are not guilty.
We shine ahead in this instant
like great hunters
and singers of old,
or the unravelers of helixes
of inspiration.
From perineum to top chakra
WE
ARE
OURS
! ! !
ALL
OF
THIS

WILL NEVER
GO
ON
forever
and gold
flashes in its birth
in the passing stream.

37

A BIRTH OF A PHOTON
is beyond redemption
as it rides on the helm of the prow
OF THE WAVE
OF ALL THINGS LEANING
on another, teetering,
back and forth, to and from
emptiness.
It is the taste
of a perfumed green curry
to be here
with the tofu and eggplant
the hot peppers and creatures
carved on the faces of matter.
All is sane as a child fingerpainting
airplanes and trees and a car.
We grow up
being fountains of tears
and spouting
unexpected laughter
but never was it better
than the mulberries
falling from
THIS TREE,
for now
we know each other
and we both have red purple
juice
on our hands and faces
and the blood of consciousness
blinks on and off swifter
than anything previously known.
Tar does that,
the whistle of the Amtrak

by the Bay
does it;
dogs bark their response
not far away
while a February orchid opens
by the cold sunny window.

38

WE HAVE ALWAYS WANTED TO DO THIS
(and who would know?)
it is like the truth continuing
TO
BE
ALIVE
and flexing deltoid muscles
in the midst of the ongoing
deception.
HERE WE ARE IN THE BEGINNINGLESS
AND ENDLESS REALM
just where the turning
WHEEL
touches the wall of stars
and clear-seeing eyes.
Everyone is with us
and you and I
are faultless
and so alone
that we shudder
like awakening cricket eggs
in the warming loam.
We are always this old and young.
The morning air
has an edge of brightness
and there is the smell
of frozen leaves
that fits into last night's
layered salmon
and rose sunset
like a black Scottish knife
into a scabbard
jeweled with crystals.
IT'S
O.K.
as the fingers of your left hand.

for Leslie and Tom

TRANSIENCY LIKE THE SHAPE OF WATER
is permanent
as the struggle of youth and old age;
looking at you is what I do,
watching your profile
slip into finer
GLOWING.
In the morning I catch myself
as I see you or I would
fall down.
If time does not come and go,
walking the cliffs is now
no larger than this moment.
The scarlet sun is flattened
by western cloud streams
above the breakers;
the children of echinoderms
cannot look up and see
the thin strands
of pelicans flying
to the roost.
Being in the depths
everything is known,
whether it is a feather
or a crusted coin
or bottle and it's understood
in the way we won't confess
TO
KNOWING.
Because we have secrets
that pull us closer
and they are not spoken.
This is how endless shape-change

creates identities
— the same ones over and over
but clad in new beings
and old loves.
It reaches into the blackest bedroom
WITH GOLDEN LIGHT
that is not there
even in imagination.

40

THE PRESENCE OF A LAUGH
is a cave lined with pictures,
and the smell of rosemary, and the call
of a red tail hawk.
Furred creatures with the robust power
of bobcats prowl,
and there is a tiny
smile at the bottom.
WE MAKE LOVE
which comes to us as bodies
and newborn pleasures.
My hand on your knee
and your deep eyes
are here with the fragrance
of lemon flowers
in winter night air;
the city glows
on one side
and the glimmer of endlessness
reflects hydrocarbons
on the other.
Myriadness whites-out
into substance
like a dark rocking chair
or a cat leaping to the deck rail.
The dragon pattern of cream
floating on thick coffee
CHANGES
to trees
and nervous systems.
Our forearms touch
and it is fine

as the smell of burning
beeswax.

Mouse eyes
watch us
and
sparkle.

41

FRECKLES OF WHITE PLUM BLOSSOMS
are older than new black boots
and enter as gases and light
AND WATER.
We are changed.
"Vain strivings tied
by a chance bond
TOGETHER."
BUT
these white petals
and yellow-tipped antennae
are our fortress
of uncountable
smiling faces.
WE ALSO ARE
this praxis of sunlight
stirring the mist,
AND
LOOK
you have sleek swimmer's arms
IN
THIS MOMENT
of Saint Valentine.
Chocolate
and fat halves of ducklings
and tiny oysters
ATTEST TO THIS
CELEBRATION
of the grandness
of
carnivory
and its aggregation
of innocent visages

I
N
T
O
the shape of our
heart's love
mirrored in nearby
grins
over the table
and reflects in the starlight
shining from pane to pane
in the glitter.

Thoreau

42

LET THERE BE MURDERS
when there are cherry blossoms
and delicate lichens
of gray-green exploring
the impossible spaces
in plain air.
THIS IS THE SAME CHILD.
IDENTICAL.
The full grown old man with a hat
and boots lives the handsomeness
I own.
This instant is good to fear dying
and disappearance.
An uncarved block
lives wholly,
ALIVE,
ALL LIVING AT ONCE
in no time, no light,
NO WHERE,
above
WAVES
at the nose of the prow.
A SWARM OF AIRCRAFT CARRIERS
barely matters
in the destruction
of Persia.
A boy making war ships
with clothespins and egg boxes
needs
GLAMOUR
and to know
the tiny glossy eyed
SHREW
is chasing a huge beetle,

and that nettle stings make welts
on young skin,
where a stream of blackberry vines
clambers over the decaying
steamer trunk.
BUT MOSTLY
the cherry-colored fire that you build
with your hands
is a river that I
step into over and over.

43

THE INTENTION OF CREATING
AN ORGANISM
of coalescing flowings
(in the beginning)
makes signs and smilings and dartings.
It is utterly merry
and spaciously still.
Moss on this chunk of redwood
is dry and ready
to burn
AND
WE
ARE FLAMING
wicks.
The darkness we shape
around us is a mare's nest
of cities, mountains,
Coltrane Meditations
and a Beethoven
string quartet,
and it is melting,
POURING,
if seen from the distance.
The myriadness of your intelligence
draws it all together
while I remember the smell
of coal buckets
and spring rain pools.
This organism
takes pratfalls
and swings its sword
into movies
hidden behind the slowness
of things. Big bursts

of sudden awareness
are
buttercups
and mallow in the field,
dripping with dew,
next to a deer scat.
Underneath it all
are capillaries and muscles.

44

THE MUSIC IS NOT SO BRIGHT
and the mind is deeper
and the layers are ragged;
at each frayed thread tip
star chambers
are woven with vernal flowers.
The chest, the shoulders, the hands,
the whole body is one tense,
ONE HUGENESS
of this moment
of meat.
Bless Francis Crick
and Odile.
Bless Freewheelin Frank
and the Frisco Chapter
of Hells Angels.
The Beauty of Aggression
IS PRECIOUS
and arrives from the same distance
AS WEAKNESS AND COMPASSION
to put the sharp teeth
that I need to love
into the soft face
SO
THAT
THUS
I learn
WHO
long dead friends are.
Meister Eckhart thinks
I allow the yellow sun cup
into me to spiritualize it
and then we are both enlarged
we are both lifted

and all else raises in complementarity.
But *up* and *down*
like *one* and *two*
are not as convincing
as the dead friends
who I love so dearly.
Only this can be done.

45

FIRE, WATER, EARTH, AIR, MEAT,
and love which we create
bask in this sun
all silky and vital
— or they are sheer smoke
scented with personalities
and cypress branches.
There are no places to go except
to the smile of causelessness
and the fleshy feet
of Eros,
OTHERWISE
IT IS ALL MURDER.
What is hidden in the raw richness
of perfection
I touch with fingertips
stroking your shapely calves.
You are a bodhisattva of kindness
and you walk through
THESE ROOMS,
this realm.
In nearby moments
hailstorms are roared
in your honor
BUT
WHAT
WE
HAVE
RIGHT HERE
on these orange petals and ashes
are beings who do not
even know
that they lack
your

COMPASSION.
Look, springtime is here
with an Easter moon
and stars
passing through.

46

I AM THE FULL GROWN OLD MAN HERE
with a hat and boots
living the handsomeness
I once owned.
It is good to fear death
AND DISAPPEARANCE
and blindness in one eye and then
the other. This moment is
ALIVE
in everything,
LIVING AT ONCE:
irreducible sexual pleasures,
muscular regrets, standing ovations,
hormones of friendship, shouting fights,
imagining mystics,
speaking with genius
and the five year old
weeping piteously for mother
IN A DARK LOW BASEMENT,
commanding his magic.
A single yellow-orange nasturtium
in full flower with petals
ruffled and rumpled —
maroon dashes and darts
around the center —
has a full quiver
of watery nectar
waiting for the child to come
and collect it
and then sip between bites
of blackness.
It's unutterably
GOOD
tasty and sweet

as I chew.
There is the flitter
of honeybees flying
round the ears
and black and amber stripes.
— Standing here
by the old
mailbox.

47

A HUNK OF IRREVOCABLE NOTHING
which taste, touch, hearing, sight,
and other senses
encase in overlapping
shimmers, interplaying
with lustrous imaginings,
makes the whiskers and skin
in the rectangular pool of glass.
Behind me
YOU MOVE
TOWARD
ME
and I am as pleased
as a lynx to be near you
((as we create each other, as we endlessly shape the other))
where the grain of sand
falls.
BUT
NOTHING
IS
as loud
and gentle as the pouring
of the silver cloudburst
on the dark deck rail.
Like the cat and the lemon buds,
this is without beginning
when we make love
and is not over
though I know the blue sky
will move toward this instant.
I imagine sunsets with you
in other realms
(but no sign of them here)
as the storm warms

the everpresent
rushing wave crest.
We know lovers
will not rest
in the whirlwind
moment.

48

FROM THE NON-BEGINNING OF THE WAVE
to the endlessness
IS A GOLDEN LION
watching the black fly
on his paw.
He is nothing and is exactly this.
His tail tip is almost still.
He is this instant:
high school shootings
and marriages and melting bridges.
WE
MAY
LEARN
that tastes of things
are imagination
overwhelmed with roadside feedlots
and rippling mounds
OF RIPE PEACHES
under the wheels of smoky trucks.
Misty walls of pink roses grow
over a house
and the rose-breasted grosbeak
sings there in his moment
and disappears.
We are in other places
but there is nothing between us
not even aircraft carriers
or roadside bombs
waiting for armored trucks.
You are wearing gray cashmere,
a black coat,
and your perfume.
There is an engine roar

in your ears.
There is the dragging grate
of earth smashing machinery
HERE
and the buzzing of the black fly.

49

THE MARCHING BAND IN THE FOREST,
the sound of jets overhead,
the whir of the washing machine
are a new breeze
in the young mulberry branches.
Carved in the consciousness
of the hiding deer,
the sun and the smells
underfoot in the grass
are also sizeless
and without proportion.
We have no containment.
You and I are this freedom
of the unstopping honks
of car horns.
It is so easy when I see
the beauty of your bare
ankles.
It is raw here
in this moment
with memories of the Caribbean
off the coast of Yucatan
and iguanas, black
on the walls
— here, where there are blue
field lilies.
LET OUR LIVES
be as sleek and singular
as a ruby-headed hummingbird
in FLIGHT.
Midair, we will draw
our tiny feet up
into the silver fluff
of our feathers

AND
we will jerk our tails
and squirt clear
fluid excrement
of the remains
of digested nectar
and midges
onto the black and green
lichen.

50

THE PURSUIT OF CONSEQUENCE
is sky blue with cracks
and blood dripping from them
and ichor and toxins and honey
and siftings of fine dust
making dunes
in the moment.
NO
PART
OF
YOU
not your wrist
or your eyebrows (or anything
of me) is touched by this
but only the quiet rain
as it falls on a candle
and the voice of freedom when there is
nothing to kiss
or not to kiss.
Incense
is of mesas and junipers
blanketed in icy hail.
Thick black toes
of the raven
on the pole
are not more present
than you and I
are, here, watching
the purple and yellow
iris blossoms
in the bright sun
of late day
in
a

world
of fog.
OUR
MEAT
IS FOR
ITSELF (OURSELF) OURSELVES.
I love you
and your veiled eyes.

51

NOTHING ABOLISHES CHANCE
and we are meat in the moment;
assemblies of incarnate flesh,
three seconds before the Bang,
build subparticles of imagination.
They are half as shapely as your naked legs
when you open
the curtains on tiptoe,
or as the cheetah (unable to conceive
of savagery) as she speeds up and closes
to pounce on the Thomson gazelle,
to turn into milk
for her son and daughter.
Together we know things
as they ARE.
The black spots
on the burnished fur
are wisdom like paw prints
on velour earth.
The white cubes clicking on baize
are no mystery
but the light above them
appears to be
in an old painting
representing a table,
or rocky stones on a path
where there are sometimes pearls
and crystal arrowheads
that appear divine.
Car horns rattle the calm
of the five petals
on
the open rose.
PINK

is all right.
YEATS
tormented himself
hoping to be brittle
and manly.

52

YOU FIND THE UNFINISHED,
CRUDE, BLACK AXE HEAD
in the redbrown dust.
Nearby, wooden bells clack
and cattle are talking.
There is the jeering and gaming
of children over the hill.
Hells Gate is in every instant
as is the featureless bland wall
OF PARADISE;
there is griffonage
and huge grafitti
on the sizeless pages of smoke
and iron — and a tree
has white flowers in the traffic
and sun by the roundabout.
THIS
IS
the shapes of our names
as they touch each other
giving a beginning to shoulders
and an end to daydreams
ABOUT SOULS
other than those made
of
a
rich life.
The home-going snails stare
with pop eyes
at delicious mold
in the shade of the cairn,
and seventeen thousand men and women,
near the coast of Persia,
live lives on a fleet

of vessels carrying planes
and missiles and helicopters
and secret biological
and cyber weapons,
and implements of penetration and radiation.

53

SPONTANEOUSLY PERFECT NOTHING
abolishes change
as does the smile on your face
in your broad straw hat
IN THE SUN
in the middle of a
universe.
This moment the cat sleeps
on the yard lounge
under a blue towel
the color of corn flowers
and there is no hail falling.
This is a perfect description
of everyone knowing
it is truth and courage
and our mammal, warmblood
nature that do nothing.
Nothing will save us
and the appreciation of it
is a necessary disguise
for feeling love or compassion.
Mindfulness is a truck tire
in the middle of the roadway
COMMANDING
ALL
THAT
PASSES.
Dreams curl up to sleep
in the afternoon
and darkness fills the empty room
much as light does
where, like music,
they are shaped by consciousness
and two-by-fours and the smell

of plaster. Plastic
can be used
to shape tiny, gleaming, scarlet
flying horses
that are sewn to children's hats.

54

LIVES IN THE MORNING AIR:
midges, flies, doves, spores,
and the sounds of a machine.
NO MORE YOU-AND-ME WOULD
be boring except for the eucalyptus trees
and the light easy fog.
The moment is our one body;
the rose-red of the car enamel
seen through the dark oak leaves
proves it all arises
AT
ONCE
and has no matter.
BEING LUCKY WE
do not care
J
U
S
T
loving the mammals
of ourselves as free
as Kenyan plains
and archipelagos of raw hunger
and laughter. Pointless,
and responsive. OH, I LOVE
YOU. Beyond the realms
of neuron-firing, awareness
roughs
itself into being
as it happens.
This old scroll of alchemy
is the newest science
and not a log cabin

for Boy Scouts.
This is countless times
BETTER
than being rich
and it has sweet breath.

55

SUBTRACT US FROM OURSELVES
and we are in the sundown light
where the week-old filly plays
with the red plastic tub,
stepping into and out of it
and moving it with her hoof.
Her slender deer-colored legs
need myriad experience
and the nerve palace
of her skull
wants to step over rocks,
through bushes and streams
and up hillsides.
Without knowing it, she needs
hunters and devourers
and high grass and stands of trees.
Let the sparking of her consciousness
not be manic or flat
as the eyes of car drivers.
BLESS
HER
POTENTIAL
FREEDOM.
Where we look
the mountain is a dark
blue-purple shape
in paler darkness.
You tell me about
the dawn chorus of the birds
and how the rooster's crow
stands out in the simple
robin songs.

WE HAVE MANES
and so does the foal.
The moments are a moment.
Salvation of all beings
is an endeavor.

56

DAZED WITH THE FANTASY
of scents of molecules, atoms, particles,
superstrings, touches of space,
energy, matter, gravity
— stuff clutching with bonds
U
N
Z
I
P
P
I
N
G
in a trillionic
swirl-dance of kalpas.
IT IS YOU AND I
with the fat black and yellow
bumblebees
supping nectar from the lavender
flowered catnip.
The rest is ripening mulberries,
some fallen
on the bricks and the moss
between them, some
in the dark churning bellies of robins.
There's no touch of known self-deception
in the peace following this noisy concord
before the morph into sunyattta,
no blockbuster curses hurled
into cold mountainous Afghanistan
OR
BEATING
of hooded prisoners.

We are curled against the nearby
soft slopes of a moment
where the endless lies make a permanent fire
to consume themselves.
We are free of the institutionalization of deceit.
Right here I can marvel
at the imagined sound of a mulberry bouncing
and own your kiss and your gaze
—while the international makers of air war machines
flaunt their products in Paris, celebrating their sales.

57

BLACK SOULS ARE CLEARED FOR VICTORY,
and spirits prepared for nada
are less than a flicker
in bright sunlight air
or the loud gloaming, wave-crash
and yowp at Whaler's Cove.
We see this so clearly
and with less registration
than the scent of mild tea.
IT
IS
TOO CLEAR
like the drippings of Jackson Pollock
before they mat into skeins.
I smile facing Leviathan and Behemoth
and see the whites
of their eyes
and their massive energetic solemnity
stilled in the huge acts
they make of their swimming
and their crashing
and it is no more than,
perhaps less
than, the simple spirits.
These are things that will never
BE CLEAR
though they are as broad as day
and can smell like ripe cantaloupe
or bones in the sun.
These are not night-happenings
but as plain
as a living thing, flying to a flower,
or to make a
kill, or to mate

with another.
Materials must be imagined
or they are
naked nothingness
in a cream-white vase
decorated
with floating blue horses
belonging to a long dead
emperor.

58

MIRACLES FULL BLOWN IN OUR FACES
and behind lead shields
is the awareness of micro-organisms.
This moment is the only alchemy
and is no more special
than a halved apricot with green at the edge
of its kernel
pretending to have the shape
that we imagine.
Sun flares down on careening trucks
spray-painted with messages.
A small snore comes from the cat
and snow falls with a soft plop
from a pine
all
at the same
INSTANT
that the cloudy scent of lemon flowers
flows into our
CAVES
in full-moon light
and billows about
our eyes and cheeks
while we breathe.
IF THERE IS A TREE
it grows like this
AS
WE
LIVE
and much much more,
in realms that are not
contrived by particles or waves
—NOT DARK,
NOT LIGHT,

AND NOT HERE—
like a field mouse or a goldfish
or a crumbled chunk of tarmac
by the roadside,
within hearing
of the winter stream.

59

WHAT GOOD MONEY OWNS US?
We laugh at the thought.
Protection is not part of the infrastructure
OF THE MOMENT,
which is pliant as a green shoot
or the lips of a pony.
IT
MUST
BE SO
or there is not a face
of freedom to smile.
THIS LIBERATES US
to gamble
the crimson tee shirt of the biker
against the coalescing uniformity
that would devour the future.
But the future owns the business
of being dangerous.
A stone has no pleasure in being forever.
I notice these things in the perfect
upper valley of your buttocks
near the lower backbone
where good feeling
comes into existence
and neurovelvet
shakes free
from the heaviness of ideas.
Poetry and philosophy
become one
unpurchaseable art.
Art and biology
hang like apples

from the trees of childhood.
And not like these manufactured
orchards of destruction.
It is the deep geology
of stars and breathing.

60

OLD AGE IN A NAZI NATION
is as good as youth in the wild,
deep-stirring music and dancing
in the swirling patchouli of lights and pictures
sliding over the body
and walls and ceiling.
The pulse thrums and hormones throb
in high-mindedness and sexuality.
Sweat drips between the pectoral muscles
and onto boots and bare feet.
Love is made with the mystic throb
of the brow.
Myriadness of mind
MUST GROW
into liberation
OF BEINGS
and
it
may
be a gift
to live for a moment
in hell worlds.
Spiritual occasions
are furnaces
burning us without smoke.
You are free of guilt and proud
and you honor this instant
with the winsomeness
of your face
as you awaken.
The Baader Meinhof Gang
has gone into hiding
with the corporations and the viziers.

Nothing is more immortal
than my kiss
on your breast.
Inside and outside are
a fantasy.

61

I REPORT THAT

EVEN DUST IS ORDINARY AS STARS AND A MOUSE
where the red skin of the madrone tree
rubs with the fog
from the ocean and city.
Tree beings' constant growth,
inseparable from awareness,
is their moment.
TINY WASPS
find
figs and branches
to change into living galls
that whisper to
passionate living flames
of the Sun's storm tides.
Plain and normal,
YOU TOO
ARE AN ORDINARY
ACTION PHILOSOPHER
brightening the realm
you read aloud in
AND
CAUSING
CHANGES OF RADIANT INTENSITY
where you walk
in this instant.
Clearly, it is a garden of all
proportions from the interstitial
dragons and dragon lovers
to the ineluctable
ineffable.
The foods we make
and eat
are charms of proteins

and oils and sugars.
This coruscates when
you move your arm and smile.
NOTHING MORE
is needed in this roar
and grind of garbage trucks
and the neighing of horses
and rare silence of
twilight.

62

THE QUEST OF CONSCIOUSNESS IS NADA
in full being,
nothing wound over and through itself
within butterfly flights and bare basements
storing unknown colors.
Discarded four-by-fours turned gray
with bent rusty nails
are in yards squeezed into their non-existent
DIMENSION
WHICH IS HUGER THAN
EVERYTHING
CAN IMAGINE.
I smell your moist back.
It is a moment
in the flutter
of worlds
AND
WE
ARE
GOLDEN
LIONS
sleeping by the roadside
in the tall grass.
Everything is stable and calm and we smile
as the discovery of awareness begins
and contradictions slip into and through
one another and kiss with large lips
and bright eyes. A tree is immobile
with leaves flexing and flicking behind phone wires.
Wild pigeons step into and out
of changing splotches of light and through
dust and pollen that settles on the hoods

of white trucks with maps and shields
on their doors showing the direct path
outwards or inwards.
The mammoth incessant city sound
could be chopped with a scimitar.

63

NO REASON TO HOLD BACK THE PARTY
everything is eaten alive
and loves it.
The received perception
OF AWARENESS
is as good as a backrub and the green eyes
of a loving cat with white whiskers.
This is a fire but we do not sit and sing
at its edge or speak of old
hunting trips.
There is no dance in the April rain
on platinum cinders.
Desperate and kind we own it all
in this cold lovely drip of water.
The melting together of our knowing
is the jewel
— a blend of emerald and ruby —
scattering light from meat.
The tiles on the bathroom floor
are highly glazed
chilling
MY
BARE
SOLES
and everywhere
are signs
of you: — your voice,
your perfume,
a blonde hair on the counter.
I know we have inner lives
because I am deeply moved
by patterns of sunlight and shade
on the withered skin of my legs
and remember

a sac of spider eggs, dusty,
covered with leaf fragments,
on the side
of a steep stone cliff
above the boulders where we walk.
Beside the creek is a deer skeleton.

64

SWIFTLY MOVING JAGGED UNRECOGNIZABLE,
pelican shadows race over
like the mottled sand cliffs and dunes
behind us—all peaked with ragged,
succulent beach rocket.
Let's wonder what things
move. Stars? and waves?
Shadows?
A reflection
from your eyes
in the morning light
sinking into silicon grains
of the littoral? Here
P
H
O
T
O
N
S
CAREEN
on the bronze-gold surface
of SUVs
and caterpillars march single file
onto the plum tree
carrying masks of hunger.
My shoulder supports your resting head
and our backs shape to
this gray log in the wind.
It is not a searching, hungry dragonfly or water strider
gliding windborne on the beach
but a bent twisted shard of brown kelp
chasing nylon
fragments.

THIS IS ALL RICH AND DULL
as only comfort can be.
The coolness around us is a moment
in our prosaic rest
staggering through paths
of red poison oak
undergrown by sage
and scarlet Indian paintbrush.
Somewhere friends have faces of angels,
looking inward and smiling;
once a sea elephant slithered
out of winter waves by that dark rock!

65

NO THUNDERING FOOTSTEPS DISSOLVE
this moment of gold and ivory
CARVED INTO TWILIGHT
and fragrant with shades
OF LAVENDER.
The smell of a boy's dreams
in a remembered museum
is here.
BUT IT IS THE LIGHT
in your eyes and the blue spark
that sets fire to my inner life
and gives warmth to good feeling.
Always your face is the visage
of a profoundly intelligent child.
Tobacco-colored hills saddled
by green oak forests
are near the unending miles
of dealers of valuable cars and trucks.
Building materials and tiles
and stones for the wealthy
pour out of a hole that bleeds petroleum.
SOME
TIMES
we know there is no need for this
and we ask to bathe in a warm pool,
and forget the origin of water.
FEELING GOOD
means we must embrace
guilt and shame
as our legacy and believe
in these bodies,

C
A
R
I
N
G
for them as deeply as we may
and must,
for Pride is a far second
to the dreams, actions, and loves
of meat.

Credits

Grateful acknowledgment for permission to print or reproduce material is made to the following publishers:

"Dream: The Night of December 23rd," from *Fragments of Perseus* by Michael McClure, copyright © 1977, 1978, 1979, 1980, 1981, 1982, 1983 by Michael McClure. "Spirit's Desperado," "Mexico Seen from the Moving Car," "The Butterfly," "The Cheetah," from *Simple Eyes & Other Poems* by Michael McClure, copyright © 1993, 1994 by Michael McClure. From "Haiku Edge": "HEY IT'S ALL CON/SCIOUSNESS," "PINK BANDAID," "MOLDY/BOARD," "BRASS," "OH,/HUM/MING/BIRD," "Hey/DRIVER," "For James Broughton/THE DRY," "THE FOX TURD," "THE HERON," "ORION," "BEFORE DAWN," "BUTTERFLIES"; from "Crisis Blossom": "grafting one," "grafting two," "grafting five," "grafting nine," "grafting fourteen," "bud," "grafting eighteen," "grafting nineteen," "flower"; from "After the Solstice": "GIVE WAY OR BE SMITTEN INTO NOTHINGNESS . . . ," "THERE'S/ME/and no me," from *Rain Mirror* by Michael McClure, copyright © 1991, 1993, 1994, 1996, 1999 by Michael McClure. Poems from *Fragments of Perseus, Simple Eyes & Other Poems,* and *Rain Mirror* used with permission of New Directions Publishing Corporation.

"A Cool Pamphlet - La Plus Blanche," "For Artaud - 8," "For Jack Kerouac / The Chamber," "Love Lion Book - Oh Fucking Lover Roar With Joy - I, Lion Man," "Mad Sonnet 1," "Mad Sonnet 13, for Allen Ginsberg," Mad Sonnet 2," "Ode for Soft Voice," "Ode to Jackson Pollock," "Poison Wheat," "Rant Block," "Yes Table," from *Huge Dreams* by Michael McClure, copyright © 1960, 1961, 1964, 1965, 1968, 1970 by Michael McClure. Used by permission of Penguin, a division of Penguin Group (USA), Inc.

Index of Titles and First Lines

Titles appear in roman type. First lines appear in italics. Poems whose titles consist of numerals are indexed by first lines only.

Text and display *Garmond Premier Pro* Compositor *BookMatters, Berkeley*
Printer and binder *Maple-Vail Book Manufacturing Group*